Adobe® Dreamweaver® CS5

Level 1

Adobe® Dreamweaver® CS5: Level 1

Part Number: 084502
Course Edition: 1.0

NOTICES

Adobe® Dreamweaver® CS5: Level 1

About This Course

You want to make information available on the Internet. To achieve this, you need to create a website. In this course, you will design, build, and upload a website using Dreamweaver.

Creating web pages using HTML code can be a tedious task. It will be simpler if you can create web pages by the click of a few buttons. Dreamweaver has some features that help you easily create and upload websites.

Course Description

Target Student

This course is intended for novice web designers, web developers, website designers, and graphic artists with some programming background who need to build simple websites and want to utilize the features of Adobe Dreamweaver CS5. The course covers the Adobe Web Communication using Dreamweaver CS5 objectives, and is intended to help prepare students to take the Adobe Certified Associate exam. Please refer to the CD-ROM that came with this course for a document that maps the Adobe Web Communication using Dreamweaver CS5 objectives to the content in the Adobe Dreamweaver CS5 series.

Course Prerequisites

To ensure your success in this course, it is recommended that you first take the following Element K course (or have equivalent knowledge): Web Design with XHTML, HTML, and CSS : Level 1.

Course Objectives

In this course, you will design, build, and upload a website.

You will:

- Identify basic web design concepts and customize the Adobe® Dreamweaver® CS5 interface.
- Build a website.
- Design web pages.
- Create reusable site assets.

- Work with different types of links.
- Upload a website.
- Work with framesets.

How to Use This Book

As a Learning Guide

This book is divided into lessons and topics, covering a subject or a set of related subjects. In most cases, lessons are arranged in order of increasing proficiency.

The results-oriented topics include relevant and supporting information you need to master the content. Each topic has various types of activities designed to enable you to practice the guidelines and procedures as well as to solidify your understanding of the informational material presented in the course.

At the back of the book, you will find a glossary of the definitions of the terms and concepts used throughout the course. You will also find an index to assist in locating information within the instructional components of the book.

In the Classroom

This book is intended to enhance and support the in-class experience. Procedures and guidelines are presented in a concise fashion along with activities and discussions. Information is provided for reference and reflection in such a way as to facilitate understanding and practice.

Each lesson may also include a Lesson Lab or various types of simulated activities. You will find the files for the simulated activities along with the other course files on the enclosed CD-ROM. If your course manual did not come with a CD-ROM, please go to **http://elementkcourseware.com** to download the files. If included, these interactive activities enable you to practice your skills in an immersive business environment, or to use hardware and software resources not available in the classroom. The course files that are available on the CD-ROM or by download may also contain sample files, support files, and additional reference materials for use both during and after the course.

As a Teaching Guide

Effective presentation of the information and skills contained in this book requires adequate preparation. As such, as an instructor, you should familiarize yourself with the content of the entire course, including its organization and approaches. You should review each of the student activities and exercises so you can facilitate them in the classroom.

Throughout the book, you may see Instructor Notes that provide suggestions, answers to problems, and supplemental information for you, the instructor. You may also see references to "Additional Instructor Notes" that contain expanded instructional information; these notes appear in a separate section at the back of the book. PowerPoint slides may be provided on the included course files, which are available on the enclosed CD-ROM or by download from http://elementkcourseware.com. The slides are also referred to in the text. If you plan to use the slides, it is recommended to display them during the corresponding content as indicated in the instructor notes in the margin.

The course files may also include assessments for the course, which can be administered diagnostically before the class, or as a review after the course is completed. These exam-type questions can be used to gauge the students' understanding and assimilation of course content.

As a Review Tool

Any method of instruction is only as effective as the time and effort you, the student, are willing to invest in it. In addition, some of the information that you learn in class may not be important to you immediately, but it may become important later. For this reason, we encourage you to spend some time reviewing the content of the course after your time in the classroom.

As a Reference

The organization and layout of this book make it an easy-to-use resource for future reference. Taking advantage of the glossary, index, and table of contents, you can use this book as a first source of definitions, background information, and summaries.

Course Icons

Icon	Description
	A **Caution Note** makes students aware of potential negative consequences of an action, setting, or decision that are not easily known.
	Display Slide provides a prompt to the instructor to display a specific slide. Display Slides are included in the Instructor Guide only.
	An **Instructor Note** is a comment to the instructor regarding delivery, classroom strategy, classroom tools, exceptions, and other special considerations. Instructor Notes are included in the Instructor Guide only.
	Notes Page indicates a page that has been left intentionally blank for students to write on.
	A **Student Note** provides additional information, guidance, or hints about a topic or task.
	A **Version Note** indicates information necessary for a specific version of software.

Course Requirements

Hardware

- An Intel® Pentium® IV processor
- 512 MB of RAM
- 1 GB of available disk space for software installation, and an additional 10 MB for the course data files
- A 256-color monitor with 1024 x 768 resolution
- A DVD-ROM drive
- Internet connection
- Network connectivity

Software

- Adobe® Dreamweaver® CS5
- Microsoft® Office 2003 or later

● Microsoft® Internet Explorer® 6.0 or later

Class Setup

1. Install Adobe® Dreamweaver® CS5.

    If you already have a full version of Adobe® Dreamweaver® CS5 installed on your computer, this course will run best if you uninstall and reinstall Dreamweaver to reset the application to the default settings. *Warning:* Uninstalling and reinstalling Dreamweaver will require you to reenter the serial number of the program. If you do not have the serial number and installation CD available, do not uninstall.

    If you are unable to uninstall/reinstall the program, you should remove the Our Global Company site, if it exists. Launch Dreamweaver and choose **Site→Manage Sites.** In the **Manage Sites** dialog box, click the Our Global Company site, if it is listed, and click **Remove.** Exit Dreamweaver.

2. Make sure that you have web browser software properly installed on your computer.

3. Make sure that file extensions are enabled. Open **My Computer.** Choose **Tools→Folder Options.** The **Folder Options** dialog box appears. Select the **View** tab, uncheck the **Hide extensions for known file types** check box, and click **OK.**

4. On the course CD-ROM, run the 084502dd.exe self-extracting file located within. This will install a folder named 084502Data on your C drive. This folder contains all the data files that you will use to complete this course.

5. On the instructor machine, install Microsoft Internet Information Services and configure an FTP server with an IP address of 172.30.4.197.

    Open **My Computer.** Navigate to the **C:\Inetpub\ftproot** directory and create a folder named Test_Student## for each student, where ## is a unique number between 1 and 25 that you will assign to each student, and a folder named Test_Student100 for the instructor. (If you have more than 25 students or less, adjust the range accordingly.)

 You can also install IIS on a separate machine to act as a remote server.

6. If the students are going to perform lesson labs in a classroom environment, then in the **C:\Inetpub\ftproot** directory, create a folder named Student## for each student, where ## is a unique number between 1 and 25 that you will assign to each student, and a folder named Student100 for the instructor.

7. The activity in topic C of lesson 5, "Creating an Email Link", requires configuration of an email account in an email client, such as Microsoft Outlook Express, on your computer

8. In addition to the specific setup procedures needed for this class to run properly, you should also check the Element K Press product support website at **http://support.elementkcourseware.com** for more information. Any updates about this course will be posted there.

List of Additional Files

Printed with each activity is a list of files students open to complete that activity. Many activities also require additional files that students do not open, but are needed to support the file(s) students are working with. These supporting files are included with the student data files on the course CD-ROM or data disk. Do not delete these files.

1 Getting Started with Dreamweaver

Lesson Time: 35 minutes

Lesson Objectives:

In this lesson, you will identify basic web design concepts and customize the Adobe® Dreamweaver® CS5 interface.

You will:

- Identify the basic concepts of web designing.

- Locate elements on the Dreamweaver interface.

- Customize the interface.

Introduction

Being a new user of Dreamweaver, you may want to familiarize yourself with its basic features before beginning to create a website. In this lesson, you will get fully acquainted with the Dreamweaver application.

Imagine using a computer without having a basic understanding of its components and operations. You may have to spend hours trying to accomplish a simple task. The same would be the case if you were to use Dreamweaver without understanding its components or their use.

This lesson covers all or part of the following Adobe Web Communication using Dreamweaver CS5 objectives:

- Topic A

  - Objective 1.1a: Identify information that determines purpose, audience, and audience needs for a website

  - Objective 1.2a: Identify criteria for determining whether content is relevant to the website purpose

  - Objective 1.2b: Identify criteria for determining whether content is appropriate for the target audience

  - Objective 1.5a: Demonstrate knowledge of the relationship between end-user requirements and design and development decisions

- Objective 1.5b: Identify page elements that are affected by end-user technical factors such as download speed, screen resolution, operating system, and browser type
- Objective 2.1a: Identify attributes of a website that demonstrate consistency
- Objective 2.1c: Identify the benefits of consistency
- Objective 2.2c: Demonstrate knowledge of BrowserLab online service for cross-browser compatibility testing.
- Objective 2.3a: Demonstrate knowledge of graphic design elements and principles
- Objective 2.3b: Identify examples of horizontal symmetry, vertical symmetry, diagonal symmetry, radial symmetry, and asymmetric layout
- Objective 2.3c: Recognize examples of page designs that violate design principles or best practices
- Objective 2.4a: List elements used to improve website usability
- Objective 5.6a: Demonstrate knowledge of HTML tags, including HTML, HEAD, TITLE, BODY, H1-H6, P, EM, STRONG, A HREF, TABLE, TR, TD, OL, LI, UL

- Topic B
  - Objective 3.1a: Identify and label elements of the Dreamweaver interface
  - Objective 3.1b: Demonstrate knowledge of the differences between Design view, Code view, Split view, and Live mode
  - Objective 3.1c: Demonstrate knowledge of the Workspace Switcher
- Topic C
  - Objective 3.6a: Demonstrate how to open, minimize, collapse, close, resize, dock, and undock panels; how to access preset workspaces; how to change document views; how to save a custom workspace

TOPIC A

Identify the Basic Concepts of Web Design

Designing a good website calls for adequate preparation. Before you begin to create a website, you need to understand what constitutes a website, and the underlying principles that govern its design. In this topic, you will identify the basic concepts of web designing.

Creating a well-designed website is as important as displaying accurate content on it. Understanding the basic concepts of web design will provide you with the proficiency to create a website that is not only user friendly and easily navigable, but also contains consistent and appropriate elements and attributes.

XHTML

eXtensible HyperText Markup Language (XHTML) is a markup language that is used to create web pages. XHTML is a reformulation of HTML that conforms to the XML syntax. It not only defines the structure and layout of a web page, using tags and attributes, but also allows you to add text and images to a web page and provides parameters that control the web page appearance.

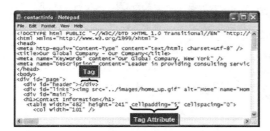

Figure 1-1: An XHTML document.

XHTML vs. HTML

XHTML is very similar to HTML but has stricter coding rules, resulting in a cleaner version of HTML. XHTML provides greater reliability and more flexible design, and results in more consistent layouts than HTML. The following table describes some differences in tagging between HTML and XHTML.

XHTML	HTML
All tags and attributes must be in lowercase.	Tags can be in either uppercase or lowercase.
All tags must have a closing tag.	Some tags do not require closing tags. For example, the <p> tag does not require a closing tag.
All tags must be properly nested. Proper nesting occurs when the opening and closing tags are completely within another pair of opening and closing tags.	Some tags can be improperly nested.

XHTML	*HTML*
All attribute values must be within quotes.	Attribute values need not necessarily be within quotes.

Commonly Used Tags

The following are a few of the commonly used tags for creating web pages.

Tag	*Used To*
`<html>`	Identify a document as an HTML document for the browser.
`<head>`	Define a container for all the elements that constitute the head section of a page. The elements include the title, meta information, CSS styles, and scripts.
`<title>`	Define the title of a web page. The title appears on the title bar of the browser window.
`<body>`	Define the body of a document. The content within the `<body>` tag is displayed when the page is viewed in a browser.
`<h1>` to `<h6>`	Format text as headings on a web page. The `<h1>` tag is used to define headings of the largest size and the `<h6>` tag that of the smallest size.
`<p>`	Present text as a paragraph with space at the beginning and end of the paragraph.
`<li>`, `<ol>`, `<ul>`	Define lists and format them as ordered or unordered.
`<em>`, `<strong>`, `<i>`	Render text as emphasized, strong, and italics.
`<a>`	Define an anchor that can be used as a link to another document or to a section of the same document.
`<table>`, `<tr>`, `<td>`	Create tables and define their rows and cells.
`<img>`	Embed images on a web page.

These tags can be used in both XHTML and HTML documents.

Websites

A *website* is a collection of web pages displayed on the Internet via a single or multiple web server. Typically, a website consists of a home page that is linked to other pages through text or images. Each website is identified by a unique Uniform Resource Locator (URL) and is maintained by an individual or a group.

Uniform Resource Locator (URL)

A *Uniform Resource Locator (URL)* is the unique address by which resources, such as computers, identify the location of a website on the Internet. The first part of the URL address indicates the protocol used to access the website. A common protocol is http, but there are several others. The second part of the URL represents the IP address of the website's location or its domain name.

Figure 1-2: A Uniform Resource Locator (URL) with the protocol and domain name.

Protocol

A protocol refers to the set of rules that govern the exchange of information on the Internet. *HyperText Transfer Protocol (HTTP)* is the standard protocol used to access websites. It is used to transfer and retrieve data from a web server.

The IP Address

An Internet Protocol (IP) address is a numeric address, such as 192.168.1.1, that helps identify a computer on the Internet. Each computer that is connected to the Internet, whether part of a large network on a university campus or in someone's home office, uses a unique *IP address*.

The Domain Name

A *domain name* is the unique textual name of a website, such as www.ourglobalcompany.com, that corresponds to the IP address of a computer. A website is usually accessed by using the domain name instead of the IP address. Domain names are easier to remember and also help users easily find a website on the Internet.

The Website Access Process

A web server makes web pages accessible to users based on their request. This process consists of the following stages:

1. The user types the URL of the website in the web browser.
2. The browser sends a request for the file to the web server through HTTP.
3. The web server sends the HTML content of the web page to the browser.
4. The browser reads the HTML content, formats the page according to the instructions provided in the HTML code, and displays it.

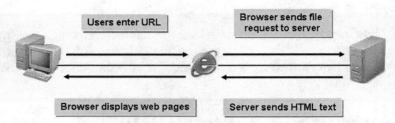

Figure 1-3: *An image displaying the website access process.*

Principles of Web Designing

Well-designed websites facilitate easy navigation through web pages for accessing the relevant information.

Guidelines

To develop a user-friendly website:

- Determine the purpose of the website.
  - What do you want the website to do?
  - Why are you creating the site?
  - Why will people come and visit the site?
- Identify the target audience who will be visiting the site.
  - Are they new or experienced web surfers?
  - What will be the demographics of site visitors?
  - What will be the connection speed to the Internet available for site visitors?
  - Will the visitors be computer savvy?
  - What will visitors want to do on the site?
- Organize the content for the website.
  - What topics or content will you have on the site?
  - Determine the content that can be grouped logically.
  - Frame a title for each of the groups.
  - Verify that there is a flow of information across groups.
- Create a layout, an outline, or a site diagram that may make navigation easier and user friendly.
  - How will the information flow?
  - How will site visitors navigate through the site?
- Standardize the text format for the web page.
  - What text and background colors should be used?
  - What should be the font size of headings and paragraph text?
  - What should be the font and font style of the text?
  - What is the paragraph format?

- Provide support for better user interactivity.
    - Provide appropriate file names for web pages.
    - Provide information on the **About Us** and **Contact Us** pages, which will be helpful for users.
    - Use feedback and contact forms to get feedback from visitors.

Example:

Global Company Inc. is a professional services firm operating internationally. The company's website aims to provide its existing clients with information about recent news and events, and also attract new clients. The target audience has been identified as predominantly other large companies. Therefore, the site can be designed to be accessed through high-speed connections. The site should have a page that lists the existing clients, and another page that provides contact details of all the firm's offices so that users can contact the nearest office for more information.

Target Audience

One of the most important factors to be clearly defined before designing a website is the target audience. This is the primary group that the site is to be designed to appeal to. A target audience can be based on specific demographics, such as gender, age, race, income, employment status, and education level. By understanding the target audience, you can provide content that is both meaningful and relevant, and present the content in such a way that it engages site visitors.

Content Relevance for a Target Audience

Content is not only the text you included on a site, but also video, audio, or interactive elements. No matter the format, content has to be results-oriented to enable visitors to retain what they gained from visiting the website. Use content that will hold visitors' attention. Don't provide too much content as the sheer volume alone can overwhelm anyone who visits the site. Conversely, add sufficient content to satisfy your audience.

Criteria for Content Presented on a Website

It is important to identify the criteria that will help determine whether the content is relevant for the website it is created for. Criteria can be determined by addressing the following questions:

- Does the use of identified content provide an added benefit to the message or goal of the website?
- Does the target audience demand such content?
- Will the content influence the file size and subsequently the download speed of the pages of a site?
- Will too much information clutter the site and dilute the message?
- What is the best media to use?

Ultimately, knowledge of your audience will guide you in presenting your content expeditiously and precisely.

User Requirements and Design and Development Decisions

In highly visible web projects where many people are involved, it can be difficult for the design and development team to pare the project down to what is necessary, what is realistic, and what is "doable" in terms of cost, timing, and resource restrictions. Additionally, when several users provide input, their needs and wants may conflict. Designers and developers have to ensure that user requirements are clearly defined, are measurable, and can be tested. The greater the clarity of user requirements, the greater the chance that the project will be a success.

Technical Factors that Affect Flash Content

There are various technical factors, such as download speed, screen resolution, operating system, and browser type, that affect web design decisions.

Technical Factors	*Description*
Download speed	Download speed is the speed at which a user's Internet connection functions. The content that is used on a website will be influenced by the download speed of Internet connections of the target audience. If the target audience is perceived to use connections with low download speed, use of videos, images, sound, and other rich media content will need to be restricted.
Screen resolution	The screen resolution will determine how a user views a web page on a browser. For example, a screen resolution of 1024 x 768 denotes that 1024 pixels are displayed horizontally and 768 pixels are displayed vertically. If the target audience predominantly uses monitors that support this screen resolution, the width of the web pages should be restricted to fewer than 1024 pixels. This will allow the entire width of the page to be displayed, without a horizontal scroll bar, when the browser window is maximized.
Operating system	Any commonly used operating system, such as Windows, MAC, or Linux, supports access to the Internet. When web pages are created, it is recommended that they are tested on different operating systems to ensure consistency in appearance across all platforms.
Type of browser	Web pages render differently on different browsers. Browsers interpret HTML and CSS code using different standards. HTML tags that work on some browsers may not work on others. Web pages need to be tested on different browsers before they are deployed on the Internet.

Design Elements

An effective web page design is the result of incorporating the standard elements of visual design.

Element	Description
Balance	Balance is the symmetry and contrast of a web page layout and its components. The use of colors and textures of images, text, and the white space that separates elements can add to or detract from the balance of a web page.
Emphasis	Emphasis is what you choose to add to a page that will give stronger attention to its message. Graphics, multimedia objects, and text styles, such as headings and background shading, can all be used to emphasize a message.
Color	Color is used to unify, separate, emphasize, and decorate. The choice of color intensity, saturation, shade, and texture are among the variations that can be used effectively in web page designing.

Violations of Design Principles

Using web design principles as a guideline to create websites will allow you to present content effectively and provide an engaging experience for users. Web pages created by web designers who violate the web design principles exhibit the following characteristics:

● Excessive content on pages resulting in lengthy pages: This requires site visitors to spend more time in scrolling through the content to seek the information they require.

● Inconsistent layout across pages of a site: Such sites are difficult to navigate through if the navigation bars are presented in different locations on each page.

● Presence of broken links and linking to the wrong pages: Links that do not open the intended page, result in users getting frustrated.

● Web pages with excessive images and rich media content: Pages with such content will download slowly, especially if targeted users have slow Internet connections.

● Images and rich media content not relevant to information presented on the site: A number of sites use images that have no relevance to the site content to decorate pages.

Elements to Improve Website Usability

Designing web pages with enhanced usability will keep site visitors engaged. The usability of websites can be improved by following this checklist:

● Use a simple navigation system.

● Use content that is clear and provides site visitors with the required information.

● Ensure that all text content is checked for spelling and grammar.

● Use images that are relevant to the context of the content.

● Keep layout and color usage consistent across the site.

● Provide options for users to search for information within the site.

● Have a mechanism for visitors to provide feedback.

●   Test the site before making it available on the Internet.

Element and Attribute Consistency

Consistency is a critical element for any website. While designing a website, it is necessary that the elements and attributes of the site be consistent across pages.

Element/Attribute	Description
Buttons	Used to create buttons that are similar in appearance. Reusing buttons across pages is a good way to ensure consistency.
Colors	Used to limit the palette of colors that you use. For example, you can use the same colors for objects that are similar.
Fonts	Used to limit the number of fonts and font styles. A site with more than a few font styles can look cluttered and be distracting.
Graphics	Used to keep the location and size of graphics similar on each page. If required, images can be reused across the pages of a site.
Layout	Every page on your site should have the same or complementary layout with elements such as the navigation bar, header and footer information, and images placed in the same location for each page.
Navigation	Used to add navigational controls to every page and keep them consistent so that site visitors can easily move to other areas of the site.
Sound	When warranted, use sound consistently throughout your site pages. If, for example, a button on one page makes a sound when visitors roll over it, you should have all buttons on all pages make the same sound.

Benefits of Maintaining Consistency

The main benefit for building consistency on a website is for user experience. If a site includes consistent elements, such as the layout and location of navigational links, the user of the site becomes comfortable and familiar with the site very quickly. Consistency is especially important for sites with multiple pages. The more you make these pages look similar, the more comfortable visitors will be while using them. This comfort level increases the odds that your site visitors will return, building user loyalty.

Layout Symmetry

Layout symmetry provides balance to a web page. A symmetrical layout can occur in any orientation and is usually divided along a horizontal, vertical, or diagonal line. A layout with symmetry has what is referred to as formal balance. A page layout with proper symmetry is visually appealing and more importantly, allows users to identify sections of a page and makes it easier for them to navigate and quickly locate the desired content.

Types of Symmetry

In addition to symmetry with formal balance, layouts can be designed with asymmetrical or radial symmetry. Asymmetrical balance is without any symmetry where there is no formal balance. Radial symmetry can use any number of axes, and it makes the image appear to radiate out from the center, like a star.

Type	Looks like
Horizontal symmetry	
Vertical symmetry	
Diagonal symmetry	
Radial symmetry	

Type	Looks like
Asymmetric layout	

CS Live

CS Live includes online features that bring the power of the web to your desktop even if you are offline. These features integrate with Creative Suite 5 applications so that you can quickly enhance existing workflows.

Service	Allows You To
Acrobat.com	Create online documents and presentations, share documents in a secured review environment, and store files remotely.
BrowserLab	Generate screenshots of your web pages rendered in different browsers and operating systems, and compare them side by side.
ConnectNow	Collaborate with dispersed working teams over the web, sharing voice, data, and multimedia.
CS Review	Publish design files, including Photoshop comp files, and enable others to quickly review and make comments on them using a number of annotation tools.

ACTIVITY 1-1
Identifying the Basic Concepts of Web Design

Scenario:
You want to create a website that provides information about your company. Before proceeding with the task, you want to ensure that you are familiar with the basic concepts of web designing.

---

1. **What does the first part of a URL indicate?**

    a) IP address

    b) Domain name

    c) File name

    d) Protocol

---

2. **Which statement is true about websites?**

    a) A website can contain only one web page.

    b) The web pages on a website cannot be linked through images.

    c) A website is accessed using its URL.

    d) Websites can contain information only in the form of text.

---

3. **True or False? Before creating a website, you need to identify the audience who will be visiting the site.**

    ___ True

    ___ False

TOPIC B
Locate Dreamweaver Interface Elements

Having identified the basic concepts of web design, you are now ready to create a website using Dreamweaver. However, being a new user of the application, you may not be familiar with the functionality of the various components of its interface. In this topic, you will locate elements on the Dreamweaver interface.

Working with the Dreamweaver application after learning its interface thoroughly will help you finish the intended tasks in an efficient manner. Also, understanding the utilities of its various interface elements will enable you to make appropriate use of them.

The Welcome Screen

The Welcome Screen is displayed when the Dreamweaver application is launched and also when you do not have any documents open. It serves as a launching pad for creating files and websites, lets you open recently used documents, and also provides links to Dreamweaver help resources. You can set your preferences to either show or hide the Welcome Screen.

The Dreamweaver Workspace

The Dreamweaver workspace consists of components that each provide a variety of tools and commands for creating and enhancing web pages.

Component	Description
Application bar	Contains menus, workspace switcher, and other application controls for changing the appearance of a document and window layout, managing Dreamweaver extensions, and creating and managing websites.
Document toolbar	Contains options that help you perform tasks such as switching between different views, previewing web pages, managing files, controlling the visual dynamics of a page, and checking web pages for accessibility standards and compatibility.
Status bar	Contains components that help in the selection of various page elements. It also provides information about the current page, such as its size and magnification level.
PROPERTIES panel	Contains options for modifying the properties of various objects, such as text and graphics, placed on the web page. The options in this panel vary based on the object that is selected.
Panel groups	Contain various panels grouped by function, such as managing files, editing HTML tags, adding dynamic content to pages, and tracking CSS rules and properties for pages. Each panel in a panel group appears as a tab.

Component	Description
Document window	Displays the current document. It is the main work area where you can insert and modify page elements.
Browser Navigation	Displays the path of the file that you are currently working on.

Figure 1-4: Components of the Dreamweaver workspace.

Guides

A *guide* is a reference line that is used to position and align objects in a document. It also helps you measure the size of page elements such as graphics. Guides can be moved, modified, deleted, and hidden. They can also be locked by using the **Lock Guides** option so that they are not moved accidentally.

Rulers

Rulers are visual aids that display graded units of measurement that appear at the top and left edges of the document window in Design view. They are used to make precise measurements of page elements and position and align layout elements accurately. The starting point of the grading on the horizontal and vertical rulers can be moved to any location within the visible portion of the ruler. In Split view, rulers are displayed only for the design section of the document window. Ruler units can be set to display in pixels, inches, or centimeters.

Document Views

Dreamweaver allows you to work with a web page in one of four views: Code view, Split Code view, Design view, and Split view or Code and Design view. Code view displays code used to create the page and allows you to manually edit the code. Split Code view splits code into two views so that two blocks of code can be viewed simultaneously in order to compare or modify the code. Design view displays a page as it would appear in the web browser, and the page is fully editable in this view. Split view or Code and Design view displays both the design and code of the page in a single window. In Code, Split, or Split Code view, the **Coding** toolbar will be displayed, which contains tools for inserting, viewing, and editing code.

Split View Options

The Split and Split Code views, by default, split the screen vertically. The **Split Vertically** option splits the screen vertically, displaying the code on the left and the design on the right in Split view. The code is displayed on the left and right in Split Code view.

When the document window is in Split view, the **Design View on Top** option enables you to display the design on the top and the code at the bottom. When the screen is split vertically, you can choose the **Design View on Left** option to display the design on the left and the code on the right.

ACTIVITY 1-2
Exploring the Dreamweaver Interface

Data Files:

index.html

Scenario:

Now that you are familiar with the basic concepts of web design, you are anxious to start creating a web page using Adobe Dreamweaver. However, you want to start your work only after familiarizing yourself with the different tools and options needed to create the web page.

---

1. Open the index.html file in the Adobe Dreamweaver CS5 application.

   a. Choose **Start→All Programs→Adobe Dreamweaver CS5** to open the Adobe Dreamweaver application.

   b. In the **Default Editor** dialog box, click **OK** to accept the default editing preferences.

   c. Observe the Dreamweaver Welcome Screen with the different sections.

   d. On the Welcome Screen, in the **Open a Recent Item** section, click **Open.**

   e. In the **Open** dialog box, navigate to the C:\084502Data\Getting Started with Dreamweaver folder.

   f. Select **index.html** and click **Open.**

---

2. **Which component in the Dreamweaver interface provides information about the magnification level of a document?**

   a) The status bar

   b) The document window

   c) The PROPERTIES panel

   d) The Document toolbar

---

3. Explore the Dreamweaver interface.

a. Double-click the **INSERT** tab and in the **INSERT** panel, from the drop-down list, select **Text** to view the various options that it contains.

b. Observe the **PROPERTIES** panel that displays the HTML properties of the page.

c. In the **PROPERTIES** panel, click **CSS,** [≡ css] to view the CSS properties of the page.

d. On the **Document** toolbar, click **Code,** [Code] to view the document in Code view.

e. Click **Split,** [Split] to return to Split view.

f. On the Application bar, click the **Layout** drop-down arrow and choose **Split Vertically** to split the document window horizontally with the code displayed on the top and the design at the bottom.

g. On the **Document** toolbar, click **Design,** [Design] to view the document in Design view.

4. **When would you use the PROPERTIES panel?**

a) To switch between different views to view a document.

b) To open a new document.

c) To view the size of the current document.

d) To modify the properties of objects such as text and graphics.

TOPIC C
Customize the Interface

Having explored the various components of the Dreamweaver interface, you are ready to work with them. Before you begin, you may want to modify the default settings of the interface elements to suit your preferences. In this topic, you will customize the Dreamweaver workspace.

While creating a web page, you may have to use certain tools and commands more frequently. Making those tools and commands quickly accessible will help you work efficiently. Dreamweaver enables you to customize and save the workspace settings based on your work requirements.

Panel Groups

Panel groups are a collection of related panels. Each panel appears as a tab in a panel group. Panel groups can be displayed in an expanded view or collapsed to icon view, making it easier to access the panels you need without cluttering the workspace. When panels are displayed in collapsed to icon view, only the panel icon and the label will be visible. You can display a panel by clicking the respective panel icon.

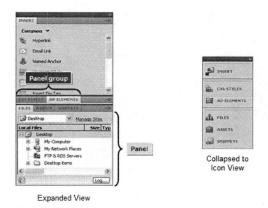

Figure 1-5: *Panel groups in expanded view and collapsed to icon view.*

The Dock

A dock is a region, usually located at the right edge of the workspace, where panels or panel groups are grouped together. Panels or panel groups can be repositioned within the dock and also moved out of the dock to float it. You can move the dock anywhere to make it a floating panel group or it can be docked to the left edge of the workspace. You can close all panels in the dock to hide it. You can restore the dock by adding a panel from the **Window** menu.

Panel Rearrangement

The appearance and position of panels can be customized by performing various operations such as docking, stacking, and grouping. The following table describes those operations.

Operation	Involves
Docking	Moving a panel or panel group into the dock on the left or right of the document window.

Operation	Involves
Undocking	Moving a panel or panel group out of the dock to make it a floating panel or panel group.
Stacking	Adding a panel or panel group to the top or bottom of a floating panel or panel group to create a stack.
Grouping	Adding a panel or panel group to another panel or panel group to create a panel group.

Predefined Workspaces

Dreamweaver provides eight predefined workspaces that aid in the design of web pages.

Workspace	Description
App Developer	Displays the document window in Split view. It has panel groups located on the left.
App Developer Plus	Displays the document window in Split view. It has some panel groups on the left as expanded panels and some panel groups on the right, collapsed to display only icons. It also has the **PROPERTIES** panel at the bottom.
Classic	Displays the document window in Split view. It has panel groups located on the right and the **PROPERTIES** panel at the bottom. It also has the **Insert** bar displayed above the **Document** toolbar.
Coder	Displays the document window in Code view. It has panel groups located on the left.
Coder Plus	Displays the document window in Code view. It has some panel groups on the left as expanded panels and some panel groups on the right collapsed to display only icons.
Designer	Displays the document window in Split view, with panel groups located on the right and the **PROPERTIES** panel at the bottom.
Designer Compact	Displays the document window in Split view. It has panel groups collapsed to display only icons located on the right, and the **PROPERTIES** panel at the bottom.
Dual Screen	Displays the document window and the **PROPERTIES** panel on the primary monitor and all panels on the secondary monitor. It is useful in a two-monitor setup.

Colored Icons

Dreamweaver CS5 displays icons in color or grayscale. By default, icons appear in grayscale but they can be switched to colored icons by using the **Color Icons** option available on the **View** menu. Panel icons also appear in color when panels are collapsed to display only icons.

The Preferences Dialog Box

The **Preferences** dialog box allows you to customize the Dreamweaver environment based on the work requirement. It contains several options grouped under different categories. These options allow you to perform tasks such as customizing startup preferences, browser settings, the functionality of code, and the appearance of layout elements.

Categories in the Preferences Dialog Box

The **Preferences** dialog box contains a variety of customization options under different categories. The following table describes those categories.

Category	Contains Options For
General	Modifying startup settings and editing preferences.
Accessibility	Prompting the user to add accessibility information for page elements, such as graphics and frames.
AP Elements	Modifying the default settings of the new AP elements that the user creates.
Code Coloring	Setting color preferences for tags and code elements.
Code Format	Formatting code, such as casing of tags, line length, and indentation for code.
Code Hints	Modifying the properties of code hints.
Code Rewriting	Specifying how Dreamweaver should rewrite code while modifying the properties of various elements.
Copy/Paste	Setting preferences for the Paste Special feature.
CSS Styles	Specifying how code that defines CSS styles needs to be written.
File Compare	Specifying the application to compare files. You need to install a third party utility to compare files in Dreamweaver.
File Types / Editors	Specifying an external editor that edits files with specific extensions.
Fonts	Setting encoding preferences for fonts.
Highlighting	Customizing the colors that highlight library items, template regions, layout elements, third-party tags, and code in Dreamweaver.
Invisible Elements	Modifying the settings of icons that indicate invisible elements.

Category	Contains Options For
New Document	Specifying default properties for new documents opened in Dreamweaver.
Preview in Browser	Setting the default browser used for previewing a web page.
Site	Setting preferences for file transfer features available in the **FILES** panel.
Status Bar	Customizing the window size and connection speed displayed on the status bar.
Validator	Specifying the language and problem against which the validator should check documents for errors.

How to Customize the Interface

Procedure Reference: Set General Preferences

To set general preferences:

1. Display the **Preferences** dialog box.
   - Choose **Edit→Preferences** or;
   - On a tab bar, right-click and choose **Panel Preferences.**
2. In the **Category** list box, select **General.**
3. Specify the desired options.
4. Click **OK** to save the changes and close the **Preferences** dialog box.

Procedure Reference: Customize the Interface

To customize the interface:

1. Open the Adobe Dreamweaver application.
2. If necessary, select the desired workspace layout.
   - On the Application bar, click the workspace switcher and select the desired workspace or;
   - Choose **Window→Workspace Layout** and then choose the desired workspace.
3. Customize the interface.
   - Hide a panel.
     a. If necessary, select the desired panel.
     b. In the desired panel group, from the panel options menu, choose **Close.**
     c. If necessary, from the **Window** menu, choose the panel name to restore the panel.
   - Dock a panel.
     a. If necessary, from the **Window** menu, choose the desired panel name to display it.
     b. Click and drag the panel to the desired location at the edge of the workspace to dock the panel.

   c.   If necessary, click and drag the panel to the desired location within the workspace to undock the panel.

● Group panels.

   a.   If necessary, from the **Window** menu, choose the desired panel to display it.

   b.   Click and drag the panel or panel group to the desired panel or panel group to group the panels.

● Stack panels.

   a.   If necessary, click and drag the desired panel from the dock into the workspace to set it as a floating panel.

   b.   Click and drag the panel to be stacked to the drop zone at the top or bottom of a floating panel.

   c.   Click and drag the panel above or below the desired panel to rearrange the panel.

● Collapse panels to icons.

   a.   On the title bar of the panel groups, click the **Collapse to Icons** button to display the panels as icons with labels.

   b.   Click and drag the left edge of the panel to reduce the width and display only icons.

   c.   If necessary, on the title bar of the panel groups, click the **Expand Panels** button to expand the panels.

ACTIVITY 1-3
Customizing the Workspace

Before You Begin:

The index.html file is open.

Scenario:

Before you start using Dreamweaver to create a web page, you would like to make some changes to the Dreamweaver interface so that you can have an interface that suits your preferences.

1. Customize the panel groups.

   a. Click and drag the **AP ELEMENTS** panel to the left and place it between the document window and the panel groups when a blue line appears between them.

   b. Observe that the **AP ELEMENTS** panel is docked between the document window and the other panel groups.

   c. In the **FILES** panel group, to the right of the **ASSETS** tab, click the gray area, and drag to the right of the **INSERT** panel, until a blue rectangle appears around it.

   d. Observe that the **FILES** and **ASSETS** panels are now grouped with the **INSERT** panel.

   e. At the top-right corner of the **AP ELEMENTS** panel, from the **AP ELEMENTS** panel options menu, choose **Close**.

   f. In the **BUSINESS CATALYST** panel, right-click and choose **Close** to close the panel.

2. Set general preferences.

   a. Choose **Edit→Preferences**.

   b. In the **Preferences** dialog box, in the **Category** list box, verify that **General** is selected.

   c. In the **Document options** section, uncheck the **Show Welcome Screen** check box to not display the Welcome Screen when the application is opened.

   d. In the **Editing options** section, check the **Allow multiple consecutive spaces** check box to create non-breaking spaces when you type two or more spaces consecutively in Design view.

   e. Click **OK** to apply the changes.

3. Save the customized workspace.

a. On the Application bar, from the workspace switcher drop-down list, select **New Workspace.**

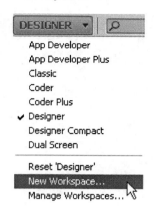

b. In the **New Workspace** dialog box, in the **Name** text box, type *My Workspace*

c. Click **OK** to save the workspace layout.

d. Choose **File→Close.**

Lesson 1 Follow-up

In this lesson, you identified basic web design concepts and customized the Adobe Dreamweaver interface. Now that you are familiar with the locations and utilities of various tools and commands in the user interface, you will be able to get started on building your website.

1. **What are the important factors that you will consider while designing a website? Why?**

2. **Which predefined workspace do you find the most useful? Why?**

2 Initiating a Website

Lesson Time: 35 minutes

Lesson Objectives:

In this lesson, you will build a website.

You will:

- Identify the elements of a project plan.
- Determine the workflow of a web project.
- Define a website.
- Create a document.

Introduction

You prepared yourself to use the Dreamweaver application. The next step is to define the structure of a website. In this lesson, you will build a website.

While creating a website, you may need to use various files of different formats scattered in a number of folders. As a web designer, you may find it tedious to repeatedly search for files on your system. Managing your files using Dreamweaver will speed up your work and also maintain the organization of the site.

This lesson covers all or part of the following Adobe Web Communication using Dreamweaver CS5 objectives:

- Topic A
    - Objective 1.6a: Identify items that might appear on a project plan
    - Objective 1.6b: Identify phases that might appear on a project plan
    - Objective 1.6c: Identify deliverables that might be produced during the project
    - Objective 1.6d: Identify common problems and issues in project management
    - Objective 2.6: Communicate with others
- Topic B
    - Objective 2.1e: Identify features used to maintain page structure and content hierarchy
    - Objective 2.5a: Demonstrate knowledge of flowcharts
    - Objective 2.5b: Demonstrate knowledge of storyboards
    - Objective 2.5c: List items that appear on a website design storyboard.

- ■ Objective 2.5d: Demonstrate knowledge of wireframes
- ■ Objective 2.5e: Recognize a website that follows the planned website hierarchy
- ● Topic C
  - ■ Objective 3.5a: Identify uses of the FILES panel
  - ■ Objective 4.1b: Demonstrate knowledge of the steps for defining a new Dreamweaver site
- ● Topic D
  - ■ Objective 4.2a: Demonstrate knowledge of the steps used to create, save, and name a new HTML page
  - ■ Objective 4.2b: Demonstrate knowledge of rules for naming HTML files
  - ■ Objective 4.2c: Demonstrate knowledge of best practices for naming HTML files
  - ■ Objective 4.2d: Identify the result of naming an HTML file "index.htm(l)" or "default.htm(l)"
  - ■ Objective 4.2e: Differentiate between document filenames and document or page titles
  - ■ Objective 4.2f: Demonstrate knowledge of how to assign a document or page title
  - ■ Objective 4.3a: Demonstrate knowledge of how to add text to an HTML page
  - ■ Objective 5.7a: Demonstrate knowledge of head content, meta tags, and tag selector
  - ■ Objective 5.7b: Demonstrate knowledge of how to add and edit head content using the Common category in the Insert bar
  - ■ Objective 6.1a: Demonstrate knowledge of how to check spelling on a web page

TOPIC A

Identify the Elements of a Project Plan

You familiarized yourself with the Dreamweaver interface in anticipation of designing a website. Now, you are ready to identify the guidelines and elements that will ensure the progress of a web design project. In this topic, you will define the elements of a project plan.

People from all walks of life plan, execute, and deliver projects that have similar phases. Though all projects have unique requirements and constraints, they usually have a beginning phase and an ending phase, with a progression of milestones in between. Each project also ends with a delivery. Similarly, a website design project plan has phases and deliverables. A well-designed project plan ensures a project's success, and smooth execution from initiation to delivery.

Project Plans

A *project plan* details how a project will be executed in order to achieve its objectives. A well-defined plan features a list of project management processes, a list of the required resources and tools, a description of the required tasks, plans for monitoring and controlling project changes, performance measurements, and a plan for communicating with stakeholders. In addition, a plan for identifying, documenting, and addressing open issues is recommended.

When managing a design and development project, such as designing websites, a plan should take into consideration the iterative nature for evaluating, redesigning, and reworking tasks.

Supporting Plans

A project plan is usually supported by other plans that detail individual components of a project plan. Commonly used supporting plans are resource plans that identify the resources available and describe their roles and responsibilities, communication plans that identify communication methods, and risk management plans that detail actions to be taken when unexpected events occur.

Communication plans are an important component of most projects. To ensure smooth progress of a project, extensive communication is required between team members, stakeholders, and clients. Team members need to be informed about decisions that will affect the development of a project. Communication with clients at regular intervals is required to keep them informed about the progress of the project and any changes that will affect the final outcome of the project.

Project Plan Phases

A complete project is often referred to as the project life cycle that extends from project planning to execution, to evaluation, and finally to launch. Projects are typically broken down into manageable and sequential phases—each with its own definitions and deliverables. For example, a typical website design process may begin by defining the audience and goals, followed by identifying the project resources. Once the resources are available, the design process will begin. After the design and storyboard are reviewed and approved, the project will move into the build and test phase. After usability is verified, the project is ready for the final phase—the launch.

Items Appearing In a Project Plan

When managing the design and development of, say a software project, such as Dreamweaver, your plan might contain the design elements, image specifications, technology to be used, resources, final output, target audience, and various other factors.

Common Problems and Issues in Project Management

Organizations spend a huge amount of money on project initiatives. The return on such investments, however, is very minimal, either the performance is poor or results are disappointing. Some of the common problems that organizations face in project management are as follows:

- Unclear goals and objectives.

- Poor communication of objectives and targets across the team.

- Unclear responsibilities across the project.

- Lack of commitment or teamwork.

- Poor planning (quality, resource, and the like).

- Unofficial *scope creep* refers to the change in a project's scope after the project work has started. An example could be addition of new features to an already approved feature list. This could delay timelines and expand budgets.

Project Plan Deliverables

A *project deliverable* is output from a project management activity that is measurable, unique, and verifiable. During the phases of the project life cycle, successive layers of detail are added to the project as it progresses. Each phase usually ends with one or more deliverables. The deliverables from one phase of a project serve as inputs to the subsequent phase. The final project deliverables require the approval and sign-off of the project stakeholders.

ACTIVITY 2-1
Working on a Project Plan

Scenario:
You are asked to work on a project plan for designing a website. Before you start on the project, you want to review the elements that constitute a well-designed project plan.

1. **Which definition best describes a project plan deliverable?**
   a) The list of resources and tools required for a project.
   b) The performance measurements of a project.
   c) The outcome of a project phase or the outcome of a project.
   d) The sequential phases of a project life cycle.

2. **Identify the plans that are used as supporting project plans.**
   a) Communication plan
   b) Risk management plan
   c) Workflow plan
   d) Resource plan

TOPIC B

Determine the Workflow of a Web Project

You defined project plans and deliverables and now you will plan the development of a website to meet specific requirements. In this topic, you will determine the flow of a project by breaking it down into a series of smaller, more manageable tasks, and then use workflow tools to define a website's intended appearance and functionality.

If you had ever tracked the making of a movie, you would have noticed that it starts by visually depicting the important characters, actions, and scenes that will form a major part of the movie and that which will appeal to its audience. This allows those working on the movie to have an understanding of its flow. This same technique can be applied to web designing. You can put all your ideas together, and define the appearance, assets, and navigation methods to arrive at a final plan for your project.

Storyboards

In its basic format, a *storyboard* consists of a series of sketches that depict the rough appearance and flow of pages on a website. A storyboard can include components denoting the use of images, navigation elements, and other important elements of a web page. A storyboard can be as simple as a few hand sketches on paper, showing the layout of pages that the user will encounter, or as complex as a full mock-up of the website. It can also be a mock-up created in another graphic application, such as Adobe Fireworks or Adobe Photoshop.

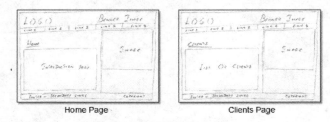

Home Page   Clients Page

Figure 2-1: Examples of customized storyboards.

Items That Appear on a Storyboard

A workflow plan, such as a storyboard, can include numerous components, each of which is translated onto the website. The location of objects that are displayed on the site pages, such as text, graphics, and multimedia objects, will be displayed in the storyboard. Objects that provide functionality in the form of navigation or user interaction are also clearly identified on storyboards. Storyboard notes describing the logical flow of projects and flowchart actions, are translated into code that provides the required functionality of the website.

Flowcharts

Unlike creating a movie, which is sequential, a website will have a different flow of action, depending on the user's input when navigating through the site. While you may have visualized the appearance of the website, it is hard to imagine the sequence of navigation based on user interaction. A more powerful and detailed way to map out the navigation flow, taking into account all interactive options, is with a *flowchart*. A flowchart allows you to visually define the navigation options on a website. You can create simple flowcharts using three symbols: start/stop blocks, process blocks, and decision blocks.

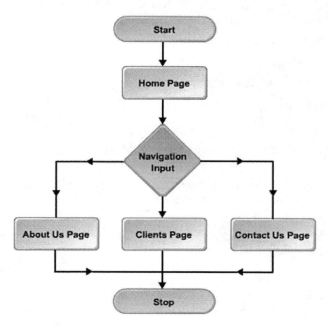

Figure 2-2: *An example of a flowchart.*

Wireframes

A wireframe is a visual representation of a website's interface. It is used to define the layout of the pages of a website before the actual process of designing the web pages. Wireframes contain information that will establish the content and user interaction. They are used to communicate the expectations of a site and develop familiarity with the site among clients and the development team. During the designing of a site, its wireframe will serve as a reference point to implement the appearance and functionality of the site.

Site Maps

A site map is a representation of the hierarchical structure of web pages of a site. It acts as a tool for defining the structure of a site, and provides references to the navigation structure of the website. It lists all the pages that constitute a website and groups the pages under clearly defined sections of the site. A site map can also be included as a web page that allows site visitors to look for and access pages on a website.

Content Hierarchy

Content hierarchy is the organization of content on a website. Site maps are a useful tool to establish the content hierarchy of a site before the process of developing the site begins. Establishing the content hierarchy of a site will allow you to identify and create content that goes into the pages of a site.

ACTIVITY 2-2
Determining the Workflow of a Project

Scenario:
While you are anxious to start your web project, you know that taking time to plan the project correctly will help ensure the project's success. Before you begin, you want to test your knowledge of the workflow tools.

1. **Which definition best describes a storyboard?**
   a) It is a visual representation of a website.
   b) It defines the navigation logic of a website.
   c) It is a series of sketches that depict the rough appearance of the pages of a website.
   d) It is a document that contains one or more sketches that depict all of the potential directions in which a website may be navigated through.

2. **True or False? A site map is an image of the appearance of a web page.**
   __ True
   __ False

TOPIC C
Define a Website

You determined the flow of a project by breaking it down into a series of smaller, more manageable tasks. Now, you will define the site structure to specify where the site files need to be stored. In this topic, you will define a website.

Initiating a website calls for the use of many files. When you have these files stored in a common location that is easily accessible, you need not waste time in navigating needlessly to locate them, and it will also enable you to create web pages quickly and efficiently.

Starter Layouts

Starter layouts are sixteen simplified layouts that are designed for cross-browser compatibility. They are listed in the **New Document** dialog box and as you click each layout in the list, the right column updates with a description and preview of the selected layout. Each Starter layout carries pre-defined navigation buttons, placeholder logo, dimensions, and specific color coding.

The Site Setup Dialog Box

The **Site Setup** dialog box is used to define a website. The **Site Setup** dialog box consists of various categories that allow you to specify the settings to define the website.

Category	Allows You To
Site	Specify the site name and the location where the file is stored.
Servers	Specify the server that will host your pages on the web. You can add or delete servers and you can also edit or duplicate existing servers.
Version Control	Specify the access, protocol, server address, repository path, server port, user name, and password.
Advanced Settings	Specify local information such as the web URL path and the default path where you want to store images. It allows you to enable cache and cloaking. The **Design Notes** settings allow you to maintain design notes and enable the uploading of the same. You can also view information about the files and folders displayed in columns and enable Contribute compatibility. It also allows you to modify templates and spry settings.

Advanced Site Setup Options

The **Advanced Settings** category in the **Site Setup** dialog box allows you to modify the site definition information. The options are grouped under different categories. This tab allows you to modify the local, remote, and testing server settings, and other site settings in addition to the options available on the Basic category. The entire site definition process can also be completed using the options on the **Advanced** category.

The Manage Sites Dialog Box

The **Manage Sites** dialog box enables you to manage sites that are defined in Dreamweaver. It allows you to edit site definition information such as the site name, the location of the local root folder and the default images folder, and other site settings. It also allows you to create a site, duplicate or delete an existing site, and import or export a site's settings.

The FILES Panel

The **FILES** panel displays a list of files necessary for the website. These files include graphics, HTML files, and other objects. It allows you to access the defined sites as well as other files on your local system. It also allows you to manage most aspects of the website, such as viewing, organizing files and links, and uploading files to a web server. Organizing the files within Dreamweaver helps you maintain the structure of the site and the links. The **FILES** panel can be expanded to view both the local and remote files simultaneously.

Maintaining a Site in Dreamweaver

When a site is defined in Dreamweaver, folder and file operations such as creating folders, and moving, removing, and renaming files and folders must be done using the **FILES** panel. This allows Dreamweaver to keep track of the location of files and update any links or references to the files when they are moved or renamed. If file and folder operations are performed outside Dreamweaver, links and references will not be updated, resulting in errors when the web pages are viewed.

How to Define a Website

Procedure Reference: Define a Basic HTML Website

To define a basic HTML website:

1. Choose **Site→New Site.**
2. In the **Site Setup** dialog box, in the left pane, verify that the **Site** category is selected.
3. In the **Site Name** text box, type the desired name.
4. To the right of **Local Site Folder,** click the **Browse for folder** icon to specify the name of the file on the local disk.
5. In the **Choose Root Folder** dialog box, navigate to the desired local root folder, which contains the files required to build the website, and click **Select.**
6. Click **Done** to define the site.

Procedure Reference: Edit the Site Definition Information

To edit the site definition information:

1. Choose **Site→Manage Sites.**
2. In the **Manage Sites** dialog box, select the desired website and click **Edit.**
3. In the **Site Setup** dialog box, in the left pane, select the **Site** category and modify the desired information.
    *   In the **Site Name** text box, edit the site name.
    *   In the **Local Site Folder** text box, specify the location of the local site folder.

 This folder stores all the images used in the site. When images from other locations are inserted into web pages, Dreamweaver creates a copy of the image in this folder and uses this copy on the page.

4. In the category list, select **Advanced Settings** and specify the settings.

    ● In the **Default Images folder** text box, specify the location of the folder, which contains the images required for the site or;

    ● To the right of the **Default Images folder** text box, click the **Browse for folder** icon. In the **Choose Image Folder** dialog box, select the desired image and click **Select.**

5. Click **Save** to modify the site definition.

6. In the **Dreamweaver** message box, click **OK** to recreate the cache for the site.

7. In the **Manage Sites** dialog box, click **Done** to apply the changes.

ACTIVITY 2-3
Defining a New Website

Scenario:

As a web designer, you are assigned the task of creating a website for your company. You created an outline for your company's website and are now ready to build it. You decide to start by ensuring that the required files to create the website are accessible from a single location in order to work on the site as a whole.

---

1. Specify a name for the new website.

    a. Choose **Site→New Site.**

    b. In the **Site Setup for Unnamed Site 2** dialog box, in the **Site Name** text box, type *Our Global Company*

---

2. Specify the settings for the site.

    a. To the right of the **Local Site Folder** text box, click the **Browse for folder** icon.

    b. In the **Choose Root Folder** dialog box, navigate to the C:\084502Data\Initiating a Website\Our Global Company folder.

    c. Click **Select** to specify the local root folder.

    d. Click **Save** to define the site.

ACTIVITY 2-4
Changing the Local Root Folder of a Defined Website

Scenario:

You were on vacation last week and your co-worker worked on the images required for the Our Global Company site in your absence. He provided you with the updated set of files for the site. Because there are changes in the images and in the structure of the site, you want to start your work with the updated set of files instead of copying only the changed files.

1. Display the **Site Definition** dialog box.

   a. Choose **Site→Manage Sites.**

   b. In the **Manage Sites** dialog box, verify that **Our Global Company** is selected and click **Edit.**

2. Change the location of the local root folder of the site.

   a. In the **Site Setup for Our Global Company** dialog box, in the left pane, verify that **Site** is selected.

   b. To the right of the **Local Site Folder** text box, click the **Browse for folder** button.

   c. In the **Choose Root Folder** dialog box, navigate to the C:\084502Data\Initiating a Website\Our Global Company - Updated folder.

   d. Click **Select** to specify the local root folder.

   e. In the left pane, select **Advanced Settings** to view the advanced settings.

   f. Under **Advanced Settings,** verify that **Local Info** is selected.

   g. To the right of the **Default Images folder** text box, click the **Browse for folder** icon.

   h. In the **Choose Image Folder** dialog box, double-click the **images** folder.

   i. Click **Select** to specify the default images folder.

   j. In the **Site Setup for Our Global Company** dialog box, click **Save** to apply the changes.

   k. In the **Dreamweaver** message box, click **OK** to recreate the cache for the site.

   l. In the **Manage Sites** dialog box, click **Done.**

TOPIC D
Create a Document

You defined a website. You now need to start creating the elements that constitute a website. In this topic, you will create a document.

The main purpose of creating a web page is to display information. Knowing how to create web pages will help you present information in the appropriate format.

File Naming Conventions

While naming files, it is better to use lowercase characters without any space, punctuation, and special characters between the names. This is because some web servers, such as UNIX and LINUX, are case sensitive and do not support special characters and punctuation. When you need to separate the words in a file name, use an underscore or a hyphen.

HTM vs. HTML

Web pages can be saved with either the HTM or HTML file extension. By default, Dreamweaver saves a file with the HTML extension. In earlier days, the HTM extension was the supported format for Windows servers that recognized only 3-character extensions. At present, both file extensions are recognized by UNIX and Windows servers.

Best Practices for Naming HTML Files

The best methods of naming an HTML file is to:

- Use lowercase characters.
- Not leave any spaces between characters.
- Not use any punctuation and special characters.

Page Size Resolution

Page size resolution refers to the number of individual pixels that a predetermined area or space on a page can contain. The standard resolution for web pages is 1024 x 768 pixels. A page size of 1024 x 768 denotes that 1024 pixels are displayed horizontally and 768 pixels vertically. At this resolution, the width of the page should be restricted to fewer than 1024 pixels. This will allow the entire width of the page to be displayed without a horizontal scroll bar when the browser window is maximized. The higher the resolution, the smaller the screen elements will appear. When a web page with low resolution is viewed on a screen with higher resolution, the screen will display empty or white spaces in the remaining area.

The New Document Dialog Box

The **New Document** dialog box contains categories from which you can create different types of documents.

Category	Used To Create
Blank Page	Blank web pages of various types, such as HTML, JavaScript, and ColdFusion. It also allows you to select predefined CSS layouts for the pages.
Blank Template	Templates of various types with predefined CSS layouts.
Page from Template	Web pages based on existing templates.
Page from Sample	Web pages based on sample pages that contain predefined elements, such as cascading style sheets, framesets, and themes.
Other	Various types of pages, such as ActionScript, C#, Java, and VB Script pages.

Document Types

The document type defines the tags and structure of the web page being created. Dreamweaver allows you to create web pages using various document types, such as HTML 4.01 Transitional, HTML 4.01 Strict, XHTML 1.0 Transitional, XHTML 1.0 Strict, XHTML 1.1, and XHTML Mobile 1.0. By default, Dreamweaver creates web pages using the XHTML 1.0 Transitional document type. Transitional document types allow usage of deprecated tags and attributes, though it is discouraged, whereas strict document types do not allow use of deprecated elements.

The Home Page

The *home page* is the entry point of a website, providing access to other pages on the site. By default, the home page is named index.html so that the web server identifies it as the entry point of the site when it is accessed using the URL of the site. If the home page of the website is referred to by any other name, such as home.html, then it can be accessed only by typing the URL of the site followed by "home.html." Using a home page name other than the default makes visitors remember the unique home page name every time they visit the site.

Head Elements

Head elements are tags that appear within the <head> tag, which includes <meta> tags and other elements that set the properties of a page. A few examples of elements that are defined in the head section of a page are page titles, background images, and text.

Meta Tags

<meta> tags are HTML tags in the head section that describe a web page. A <meta> tag can include information, such as keywords, descriptions, and character sets. This information is invisible to viewers while they are browsing, but can be used by web server software applications to pick up the page and display it in the search results.

The keywords meta tag allows you to define certain descriptive words specific to your site. These words will be indexed by search engine spiders and will enable prospective viewers to find your site during web searches. For example, a keyword meta tag will appear in Code view as `<meta name="Keywords" content="Consultation, Project, Services">`.

The description meta tag allows you to include a short description on your site. You can use it to expand on keywords. For example, a description meta tag will appear in Code view as `<meta name="Description" content="Fastest growing project management and consulting company">`. While the keywords will help your site come up in response to a search containing matching keywords, the description is part of the search engine results that users see.

Document Titles vs. Document File Names

A document title is included in the head section of an HTML document using the `<title>` tag. The document title is displayed on the title bar of the browser window. It is also used when a page is added as a favorite in a browser.

A document file name is the name that the document is saved in. Document names are not displayed anywhere within the document when the document is viewed in a browser, but they constitute a part of the URL when the page is accessed over the Internet.

The Check Spelling Command

The **Check Spelling** command in Dreamweaver allows you to check the text content in a document for spelling errors. This command opens the **Check Spelling** dialog box in which words with unrecognized spellings and suggestions of replacement words are displayed. You can choose to replace a word with any of the suggestions, type your own replacement word, and add words to a personal dictionary to avoid having them displayed as misspelled words. The dialog box also allows you to ignore or change words that are identified as misspelled.

LILO, which stands for Linguistic Library Optimized, is a shared library in certain Adobe applications that makes it possible to add linguistic services, such as spelling and hyphenation, supplied by third-party linguistic-service providers. It supports a number of languages. The default dictionary will match the installed version of Dreamweaver CS5.

How to Create a Document

Procedure Reference: Create a Web Page

To create a web page:

1. Choose **File→New.**

2. In the **New Document** dialog box, specify the desired page type and layout.

3. Click **Create** to create the web page.

4. In the document window, add the desired content.

5. If necessary, copy the content from the desired source and paste it in Dreamweaver.

6. On the **Document** toolbar, in the **Title** text box, type a title for the page.

7. If necessary, insert the head elements.

   a. Display the dialog box for the desired head element.

      - Choose **Insert→HTML→Head Tags** and then from the submenu, choose the desired command to insert a head element or;

      - In the **INSERT** panel, click **Head** and select the desired option.

   b. In the dialog box displayed for the head element, specify the desired information and click **OK.**

8. Choose **File→Save.**

9. In the **Save As** dialog box, navigate to the desired folder.

10. In the **File name** text box, click and type the desired file name.

11. Click **Save** to save the web page.

ACTIVITY 2-5
Creating a Document

Data Files:

Welcome.txt

Before You Begin:

1. Navigate to the C:\084502Data\Initiating a Website\Our Global Company - Updated folder and open the Welcome.txt file in Notepad.

2. Switch to the Adobe Dreamweaver CS5 application.

Scenario:

You are ready to start working on the web pages for your company's website. As the first step, you decide to include the basic information about the company on the web page.

---

1. Create a blank web page.

   a. Choose **File→New**.

   b. In the **New Document** dialog box, verify that the **Blank Page** category is selected, and in the **Page Type** list box, verify that **HTML** is selected.

   c. In the **DocType** drop-down list, verify that **XHTML 1.0 Transitional** is selected and click **Create** to create a blank HTML document.

---

2. Add text to the web page.

   a. Switch to the Welcome.txt file.

   b. Choose **Format→Word Wrap** to view all the content.

   c. Choose **Edit→Select All** to select all the content in Notepad.

   d. Choose **Edit→Copy** to copy the content.

   e. Switch to the Adobe Dreamweaver CS5 application.

   f. Choose **Edit→Paste** to paste the content in the document window.

---

3. Add the page title.

   a. On the **Document** toolbar, in the **Title** text box, click and drag over the text "Untitled Document," to select the text.

   b. Type *Our Global Company* and press **Enter**.

---

4. Include metadata keywords and a description for the web page.

   a. Choose **Insert→HTML→Head Tags→Keywords**.

   b. In the **Keywords** dialog box, in the **Keywords** text box, type *Our Global Company, New York*

---

   c.   Click **OK** to insert the keywords.

   d.   Choose **Insert→HTML→Head Tags→Description.**

   e.   In the **Description** dialog box, in the **Description** text box, type *Leader in providing consulting services*

   f.   Click **OK** to insert the description.

   g.   On the **Document** toolbar, click **Code** to switch to Code view.

   h.   Verify that the keywords and description are displayed in `<meta>` tags within the `<head>` tag.

   i.   On the **Document** toolbar, click **Design** to switch to Design view.

5. Save the web page.

   a.   Choose **File→Save.**

   b.   If necessary, in the **Save As** dialog box, navigate to the C:\084502Data\Initiating a Website\Our Global Company - Updated folder.

   c.   In the **File name** text box, type *index*

   d.   Click **Save** to save the web page.

   e.   Choose **File→Close** to close the web page.

   f.   Close the Welcome.txt file.

Lesson 2 Follow-up

In this lesson, you built a website. Defining the website structure in Dreamweaver will help you speed up your work and maintain the organization of your site.

1.   **How is defining a site helpful to you? What are the various options that you will set while defining a site?**

2.   **What are the folders that you will create while defining your website?**

3 | Designing Web Pages

Lesson Time: 1 hour(s), 40 minutes

Lesson Objectives:

In this lesson, you will design web pages.

You will:

● Define the basic concepts of Cascading Style Sheets (CSS).

● Format a web page.

● Identify copyright and citation requirements.

● Insert images.

● Insert tables.

● Import data from other applications.

● Organize files and folders.

Introduction

You created a web page. You may now want to enhance its appearance and add more design elements. In this lesson, you will design and modify web pages with formatting and images.

With accessibility to the Internet increasing everyday, a website is an ideal tool for presenting information to a global audience. Using suitable page elements and content is an effective way to present information. Dreamweaver provides various options to format web pages and add elements quickly and efficiently.

This lesson covers all or part of the following Adobe Web Communication using Dreamweaver CS5 objectives:

● Topic A

■ Objective 2.1d: Identify benefits of using CSS styles

■ Objective 5.8c: Demonstrate knowledge of the advantages of using CSS for design

● Topic B

■ Objective 2.4b: Demonstrate knowledge of text formatting guidelines that improve readability

■ Objective 3.2a: Identify types of content that can be created or inserted by using the Insert bar

- Objective 3.2b: Demonstrate knowledge of how to change between the categories on the Insert bar
- Objective 3.2c: Demonstrate knowledge of how to toggle between "Show as Tabs" and "Show as Menu" on the Insert bar
- Objective 3.3a: Demonstrate knowledge of the various functions of the PROPERTIES panel
- Objective 5.1a: Identify document properties that can be set or edited globally by using the Page Properties dialog box
- Objective 5.1b: Demonstrate knowledge of how to set or modify global page properties and global CSS styles, including those for text, links, and background
- Objective 5.1c: Differentiate the uses of global CSS rules and CSS rules for div tags.
- Objective 5.2a: Demonstrate knowledge of how to insert a div tag in standard mode
- Objective 5.2e: Demonstrate knowledge of how to modify div tag attributes
- Objective 5.2h: Demonstrate knowledge of how to create CSS rules in the PROPERTIES panel
- Objective 5.2i: Demonstrate knowledge of how to define, modify, and check CSS rules
- Objective 5.3a: Demonstrate knowledge of fonts, including what viewers see if they do not have the selected font installed or if "Default Font" is selected as the font type
- Objective 5.3b: Demonstrate knowledge of how to change the font, font size, and color
- Objective 5.3c: Demonstrate knowledge of how to apply a paragraph style to a paragraph of text
- Objective 5.3d: Demonstrate knowledge of how to indent text to set off a block quotation
- Objective 5.3c: Demonstrate knowledge of how to align paragraphs
- Objective 5.3d: Demonstrate knowledge of ordered, unordered, and definition lists
- Objective 5.3e: Demonstrate knowledge of how to create unordered and ordered lists and how to set properties for a list by using the List Item button in the PROPERTIES panel
- Objective 5.3f: Demonstrate knowledge of ordered, unordered, and definition lists.
- Objective 5.3g: Demonstrate knowledge of how to create unordered and ordered lists and how to set properties for a list by using the List Item button in the Property inspector.
- Objective 5.3h: Demonstrate knowledge of how to create definition lists
- Objective 5.3i: Demonstrate knowledge of how to apply emphasis to text by using the Insert menu or the PROPERTIES panel
- Objective 5.3j: Demonstrate knowledge of how to create a custom font stack using the Edit Font list command in the PROPERTIES panel or for the font-family property in the CSS rule definition dialog box
- Objective 5.8b: Demonstrate knowledge of how to use CSS to set properties for text and HTML tags
- Objective 6.1c: Demonstrate knowledge of how to preview a web page in a browser

- Topic C
    - Objective 1.3a: Use copyright terms correctly, such as "copyrighted," "fair use doctrine," "intellectual property," and "derivative works"
    - Objective 1.3b: Identify when permission must be obtained to use copyrighted material
    - Objective 1.3c: Identify methods used to indicate content as copyrighted
    - Objective 1.3d: Recognize proper methods for citing websites, images, sounds, video, and text from the Internet
- Topic D
    - Objective 4.4a: Demonstrate knowledge of the steps for inserting images
    - Objective 4.4b: Demonstrate knowledge of how to add alternative text to images by using the Image Tag Accessibility Attributes dialog box or the PROPERTIES panel
    - Objective 4.4c: Identify image file types that can be viewed in all browsers
    - Objective 4.4d: Demonstrate knowledge of image file types and their uses
    - Objective 5.4a: Demonstrate knowledge of the capabilities and limitations of editing or modifying images in Dreamweaver
    - Objective 5.4b: Demonstrate knowledge of how to scale an image
    - Objective 5.4c: Demonstrate knowledge of editing static and interactive assets with Fireworks, Photoshop, and Flash from inside Dreamweaver
- Topic E
    - Objective 4.9b: Demonstrate knowledge of table, cell, row, and column properties
    - Objective 4.9c: Demonstrate knowledge of how to set and change table, cell, row, and column properties
    - Objective 4.9d: Demonstrate knowledge of sizing methods used for tables
    - Objective 4.9e: Demonstrate knowledge of how to insert and delete columns and rows
    - Objective 4.9f: Demonstrate knowledge of how to merge and split cells
- Topic F
    - Objective 4.9a: Demonstrate knowledge of how to import tabular data
    - Objective 4.10a: Demonstrate knowledge of how to add Word or Excel content to a web page
    - Objective 4.10b: Demonstrate knowledge of the correct settings to use when importing a Word document, based on the content in the document
    - Objective 4.10c: Demonstrate knowledge of how to link to a Word or Excel document from a web page

TOPIC A

An Introduction to Cascading Style Sheets

You created a web page. Before you format a web page, you need to understand the different ways to apply formatting to page elements. In this topic, you will determine how Cascading Style Sheets can be used to format web pages.

While designing a web page, you may need to control the appearance of content by assigning text properties, colors, and font styles. Knowing the features and benefits of CSS will enable you to apply formatting to a web page and maintain a consistent look throughout the website.

Cascading Style Sheets

Cascading Style Sheets (CSS) are a collection of rules that define the style applied to specific elements. These rules determine the layout and appearance of the elements on a web page. CSS can be placed in a location different from that of the content being formatted. In this way, CSS separates content from presentation, allowing you to modify styles in one place and update all related content automatically.

Benefits of Cascading Style Sheets

CSS separates content from presentation, allowing you to modify styles in one place and update all related content automatically. Moreover, usage of CSS saves a lot of time on designing the layout and appearance of the elements on a web page, and also in maintaining the consistency of the elements across pages.

Types of CSS

There are three types of CSS: inline, embedded, and external. The following table describes the different types of CSS.

Type	Description
Inline	Applied directly to tags on a web page using the style attribute. These rules affect only the individual tags they are applied to.
Embedded	Defined in the head section using the `<style>` tag. These rules affect the tags they are applied to throughout the web page on which they are defined. They are also called internal styles.
External	Defined in a separate file and saved with the .css extension. These rules affect all the pages they are attached to, and can be linked to any web page.

CSS Rules

A *CSS rule* describes the style that is applied to an element on a web page. It is made up of two parts: the selector and the declaration block. The selector identifies the element that the rule applies to, while an individual declaration in the declaration block consists of a property and a value assigned to it. A CSS rule can have multiple declarations.

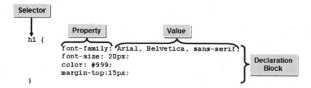

Figure 3-1: A CSS rule for the h1 tag.

CSS Best Practices

When using CSS, it is recommended to follow guidelines that will allow you to write effective CSS code. Some of the best practices of CSS coding are as follows:

- Include CSS styles in a readable format. It is recommended to create style sheets with all properties in a single line or on individual lines.
- Follow consistent naming conventions for styles in order to easily locate them and identify their usage.
- Organize style sheets into logical groups.
- Add comments, wherever necessary, for better understanding and recollection.
- Organize the properties within a style definition either alphabetically or logically.
- Decide on the type of CSS—inline, embedded, or external—based on the usage of the style across the pages of a website.
- Specify units for all properties that are measurement oriented.

Tag Styles

Tag styles are CSS styles applied to a particular tag on a web page. When applied to a tag, they modify the appearance of the content within the tag. The formatting specified by a tag style is applied when the associated HTML tag is used on a web page. The tag style can be defined in either an embedded style sheet or in an attached external style sheet.

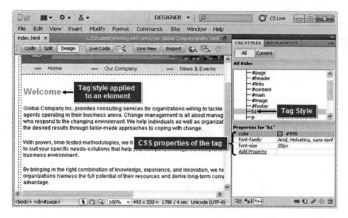

Figure 3-2: A tag style defined and applied to a web page element.

Class Styles

Class styles are CSS styles that can be applied to any element on a web page, regardless of the HTML tags being used. Class styles are identified by names prefixed with a dot, and can be defined either in an embedded style sheet or in an attached external style sheet. Class styles are applied to an element using the class attribute to which the `class` name is assigned. They are the default style that Dreamweaver creates when you create a CSS rule.

```
Class name begins    →  .thead {background-color: #B6D9EF;
 with a period                text-align: center;
                              height: 20px;
                              font-weight: bolder;
                              font-size: 14px;
                       }

                       <td class="thead">Location</td>

                            Class style applied
                              to an element
```

Figure 3-3: *A class style definition and its usage.*

ACTIVITY 3-1

Understanding Cascading Style Sheets

Scenario:

You are creating web pages and you need to apply formatting to enhance the appearance of the pages. Before you do that, you want to ensure that you can recall the various types of CSS and CSS styles that can be used.

---

1. **What is an embedded style?**

   a) A type of CSS that is defined in the head section using the <style> tag.

   b) A set of class styles that can be applied to any element on a page.

   c) A type of CSS that is applied directly to tags on a web page using the style attribute.

   d) A CSS file that is attached to a web page.

---

2. **What is a tag style?**

   a) A CSS style that is saved as a separate CSS file and attached to a web page.

   b) A CSS style that can be applied to a particular tag on a page.

   c) A CSS style that can be applied to multiple elements on a page.

   d) A CSS style that can be applied directly to tags on a web page using the style attribute.

---

3. **Which of these are types of CSS?**

   a) Inline style

   b) Class style

   c) Embedded style

   d) External style

TOPIC B
Format a Web Page

You created a web page and are now ready to enhance the appearance of the page. In this topic, you will format a web page.

You may want to direct the user's attention to specific details on the web page you create. Or, you may want to break the monotony across the various pages of textual content on your website. The various formatting options available in Dreamweaver will help you present attractive and legible content to your site visitors.

Text Properties

The appearance of text on a web page can be enhanced by modifying the various properties associated with it. The text properties that can be modified include indenting, paragraph format, alignment, font type, font style, and font color. You can modify these properties using the **PROPERTIES** panel or the **Format** menu.

CSS and HTML Properties in the PROPERTIES Panel

The **PROPERTIES** panel can be used to modify the CSS and HTML properties of page elements. In Adobe Dreamweaver CS5, the CSS and HTML properties are displayed separately.

Font Types

Dreamweaver allows you to set the font type for text selected in Design view using the **PROPERTIES** panel or the **Format** menu. Font types that can be set are families of fonts, which are commonly available on most computers. When the page is viewed in a browser, text is displayed in a font from the specified family. You can edit the list of fonts that can be assigned to text to add more fonts that can be used on your web pages.

Font type for text can also be set to **Default Font.** This will cause previously applied fonts to be removed and will apply the default font of the tag to the text. When viewed in a browser, text with the **Default Font** setting is viewed in the default font of the browser.

If a font that has been used on a web page is not available on a user's computer, text on the page is displayed in the default font of the browser. The **Edit Font List** dialog box allows you to add or remove font sets from the font list. The **Edit Font List** dialog box can be displayed by using the **Edit Font List** command in the **Font** drop-down list in the **PROPERTIES** panel.

Guidelines for Setting Text Properties

Because various factors can affect the readability of text, designers have to strike a balance between esthetics and readability when choosing the font, size, type, and color of the text. The general guidelines for text properties are as follows:

* Font type: Use fonts, such as Arial, Times, Comic Sans MS, Georgia, Courier New, Trebuchet MS, and Verdana, which are commonly available across platforms. Use sans-serif fonts such as Arial or Verdana for headings, subheadings, and captions, and serif fonts such as Times or Georgia for paragraph text as these fonts are commonly used for enhancing their clarity and readability.

* Font size: Like font type, font size will also enhance better readability. A font that is too small or too big may fail to solicit readers' attention. Using the right size for text throughout the document can help maintain consistency. Font size can vary for elements such as titles and subheadings and highlighted and lead-in text.

- Font color: The color of the font needs to be chosen on the basis of the background color. Use dark-colored text on light-colored backgrounds and vice versa for better readability.

There are a few additional tips that developers can use to increase the readability and visual appearance of text.

- Use reasonable chunks of content.
- Use limited number of fonts.
- Use bold, italics, and capitalization wisely.
- Avoid using ALL CAPITALS for every text (It is considered rude.).
- Avoid lengthy sentences.
- Avoid blinking and moving text.

Lists

Lists are used to organize and display information in a structured format. Dreamweaver provides three types of lists: unordered, ordered, and definition. In an unordered list, each item is preceded by a bullet; in an ordered list, by a number or a letter of the alphabet, and in a definition list, alternate paragraphs are formatted as a term followed by its definition. The term is left aligned with its corresponding definition left indented below it.

List Properties

The **List Properties** dialog box allows you to specify the HTML properties of list items. The attributes that can be set in HTML are the list type and its style. The two types of list types available are the unordered list and the ordered list. For unordered lists, the bullet style can be set to display a bullet or square. For ordered lists, the bullet style can be set to display numbers, roman numerals, or letters of the alphabet. Additionally, you can also specify the start count value for the list items in an ordered list.

List properties can also be set using CSS styles. CSS properties that can be set for lists are the bullet style, bullet image, and position. These properties can be set in the **CSS STYLES** panel or using the **CSS Rule definition** dialog box.

The CSS STYLES Panel

The **CSS STYLES** panel displays CSS rules that are applied to the elements on the current web page. It lets you create, edit, and delete CSS rules. It also permits you to work on CSS rules in two modes: All mode and Current mode. In All mode, the panel displays the CSS rules applied to every element on the current page; however, in Current mode, it only displays the CSS rules applied to the currently selected element. The panel also lets you attach an external style sheet to a web page.

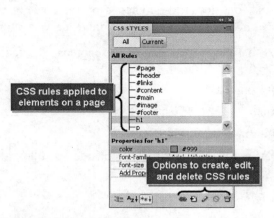

Figure 3-4: *The CSS STYLES panel in All mode.*

CSS Text Properties

CSS text properties are defined as CSS rules that affect the appearance of text on a web page. You can create these rules using the **CSS Rule definition** dialog box and modify them using the **PROPERTIES** or **CSS STYLES** panel. The **PROPERTIES** panel allows you to modify the more commonly used CSS text properties, whereas the **CSS STYLES** panel lists all the CSS text properties that can be modified. CSS text properties are chiefly categorized as **Type** and **Block**.

Category	Description
Type	Contains properties to define font attributes such as the font family, font size, color, font style, line height, font weight, font variant, text decoration, and text transform.
Block	Contains properties to define paragraph formatting attributes such as word spacing, letter spacing, text alignment, vertical alignment, text indent, whitespace, and the display style.

The Page Properties Dialog Box

The **Page Properties** dialog box is used to modify the settings of an entire web page. With the dialog box, you can set CSS properties that help modify the appearance of a page. You can set HTML properties to modify the background image, background color, text color, link styles, and margin styles of a page. It also allows you to specify a title and set the document type and the encoding method for the web page. In addition, you can define the link style and the heading style of a page can be set.

 CSS properties generated through the **Page Properties** dialog box are defined in an embedded style sheet on the page.

CSS Disable-Enable

CSS properties can be disabled or re-enabled using the **Disable/Enable CSS Property** option in the **CSS STYLES** panel. Disabling a CSS property will not delete the property, but will only disable the specified property.

The div and span Tags

`<div>` tags are block-level elements used to define logical sections on a web page. Styles can be assigned not only to these tags but also to other tags contained within. `<span>` tags are inline elements used to format other inline elements, such as text, without introducing a new block-level element.

```
<div id="main">
    <h1>Welcome</h1>
    <p><span class=highlight>Global Company Inc.</span>
provides consulting services for organizations willing to
tackle the change agents operating in their business
arena. Change management is all about managing people, who
respond to the changing environment.</p>
</div>
```

Figure 3-5: A <span> tag within a <div> tag.

CSS for Formatting vs. CSS for Layout

CSS is used on web pages for formatting content and for defining the layout of web pages. CSS styles defined for specifying the appearance of text are an example of using CSS for formatting. These style sheets can be applied to text across the pages of a site or to individual text elements on pages. CSS styles can also be defined and used along with `<div>` tags to define the structure of a web page. This allows you to create block elements on a page. Each block can be positioned using CSS properties, and the block can hold text or images.

The INSERT Panel

The **INSERT** panel is used to insert objects onto a web page. Options in this panel are categorized based on their function. The following table describes the categories available.

Category	Description
Common	Contains options to insert commonly used objects, such as hyperlinks, tables, and images.
Layout	Contains options to insert layout elements, such as frames, tables, *spry interface widgets*, and `<div>` tags.
Forms	Contains options to insert forms, form elements, and spry form validation widgets.
Data	Contains options to insert data objects, such as spry data set controls, record sets, and repeating regions.
Spry	Contains options to insert spry data set controls, spry validation objects, and spry interface widgets.

Category	Description
InContext Editing	Contains options to insert InContext editing elements such as repeating and editable regions.
Text	Contains options to modify the text properties and insert lists and special characters.
Favorites	Contains an option to add shortcuts to the frequently used options from other categories.

Display INSERT Panel as INSERT Bar

Unlike other panels in Dreamweaver, you can drag the **INSERT** panel out of its default dock position and drop it into a horizontal position at the top of the Document window. When you do so, it changes from a panel to **INSERT** bar. The **INSERT** bar can be shown either as a tab and a menu.

- Click the arrow beside the category name on the left end of the Insert bar, and then select **Show as Tabs** to show the **INSERT** bar as a tab.

- Right-click a category tab in the Insert bar, and select **Show as Menus** to show the **INSERT** bar as a menu.

How to Format a Web Page

Procedure Reference: Format Text on a Web Page

To format text on a web page:

1. Select the desired text.

    - Click and drag over the desired text to select the text or;
    - Click before the text, hold down **Shift,** and click after the text.

2. Format the text.

    - Apply formatting using the **PROPERTIES** panel.
        - Click **HTML** and set the desired HTML text properties.
        - Click **CSS** and set the desired CSS text properties.
    - From the **Format** menu, choose the property to display the desired submenu and then choose the desired text property to apply it.

3. Set the alignment of text.

    - Align text using the **PROPERTIES** panel.
        a. If necessary, in the **PROPERTIES** panel, click **CSS.**
        b. If necessary, create a CSS rule.
        c. Set the alignment of text.
            - Click **Align Left** to align text with the left border of the page.
            - Click **Align Center** to align text to the center of the page.
            - Click **Align Right** to align text with the right border of the page.
            - Click **Justify** to align a paragraph of text with the left and right borders of the page or;
    - Choose **Format→Align** and choose an alignment command.

4. Apply a paragraph style.
    *   Apply paragraph styles using the **PROPERTIES** panel.
        a. If necessary, in the **PROPERTIES** panel, click **HTML**.
        b. From the **Format** drop-down list, select a paragraph style.
    *   Choose **Format→Paragraph Format** and choose a paragraph style.

Setting Font Properties

The font properties that can be set using the **PROPERTIES** panel are font style, size, color, alignment, and bold and italic formatting. These properties can also be set using the **Format** menu. Text can be emphasized by applying the bold or italic formatting to it.

The paragraph styles that can be applied to text are **Paragraph, Heading 1, Heading 2, Heading 3, Heading 4, Heading 5, Heading 6,** and **Preformatted Text.**

Indenting Text to Create a Block Quotation

Dreamweaver allows you to create block quotations using the indent options in the **PROPER-TIES** panel and on the **Format** menu. Indenting text allows you to set text apart from the paragraph flow of a page to create a block quote. Dreamweaver inserts the `<blockquote>` tag when text is indented.

Procedure Reference: Remove Space Between Paragraphs

To remove space between paragraphs:

1. In Design view, click to set your cursor to the left of the text to remove unnecessary spacing between paragraphs.
2. Press **Backspace.**

Procedure Reference: Create a List

To create a list:

1. Select the desired text.
2. In the **PROPERTIES** panel, click **HTML**.
3. Create an unordered list.
    *   In the **PROPERTIES** panel, click the **Unordered List** button or;
    *   Choose **Format→List→Unordered List.**
4. Create an ordered list.
    *   In the **PROPERTIES** panel, click the **Ordered List** button or;
    *   Choose **Format→List→Ordered List.**
5. Choose **Format→List→Definition List** to create a definition list.

Procedure Reference: Create a CSS Rule

To create a CSS rule:

1. If necessary, choose **Window→CSS Styles** to display the **CSS STYLES** panel.
2. Display the **New CSS Rule** dialog box.
    *   Open the **New CSS Rule** dialog box using the **PROPERTIES** panel.
        a. If necessary, in the **PROPERTIES** panel, click **CSS**.
        b. If necessary, from the **Targeted Rule** drop-down list, select **<New CSS Rule>.**

     c.   Click **Edit Rule.**

- At the bottom of the **CSS STYLES** panel, click the **New CSS Rule** button or;
- From the **CSS STYLES** panel options menu, choose **New.**

3.   From the **Selector Type** drop-down list, select the desired option.

4.   If necessary, from the **Selector Name** drop-down list, select the desired tag or selector.

5.   From the **Rule Definition** drop-down list, select the location where the styles are to be saved.

- Save the CSS rule in an external style sheet.

    a.   Select the **New Style Sheet File** option.

    b.   In the **New CSS Rule** dialog box, click **OK.**

    c.   If necessary, in the **Save Style Sheet File As** dialog box, navigate to the desired folder.

    d.   In the **File name** text box, type the name of the style sheet and click **Save.**

    e.   If necessary, in the **Dreamweaver** message box, click **OK.**

- Select the **This document only** option and click **OK.**

6.   In the **CSS Rule definition for <rule name>** dialog box, in the **Category** list box, select the desired category.

7.   In the selected category, set the values for the desired properties.

8.   Click **Apply** to add the CSS rule to the **CSS STYLES** panel.

9.   Click **OK.**

Procedure Reference: Edit a CSS Rule

To edit a CSS rule:

1.   In the **CSS STYLES** panel, in **All** mode, select the desired CSS rule.

2.   If necessary, click **Current** to display the CSS styles applied to the currently selected element.

3.   If necessary, click **All** to switch to **All** mode.

4.   In **All** mode, change the CSS rule definition.

- In the **Properties** pane, edit the value of the desired properties or;
- Make necessary changes using the **CSS Rule definition for <rule name>** dialog box.

    a.   Display the **CSS Rule definition for <rule name>** dialog box.

- Right-click the CSS rule and choose **Edit.**
- Double-click the CSS rule.
- Select the CSS rule and from the **CSS STYLES** panel options menu, choose **Edit** or;
- Select the CSS rule and at the bottom of the **CSS STYLES** panel, click the **Edit Rule** button.

    b.   In the **Category** list box, select the desired category.

    c.   Update the values of the desired properties.

    d.   Click **Apply** and click **OK** to apply the changes.

CSS Properties for <div> Tags

When defining a CSS rule for applying it to a <div> tag, the properties that can be specified determine the position, size, and appearance of the div element on the web page. Some of the commonly used properties for <div> tags are box properties such as width, height, padding, and margin; border properties such as style, width, and color; and positioning properties such as top, right, bottom, left, and positioning method.

Procedure Reference: Add Head Content Using the INSERT Panel

To add head content using the **INSERT** panel:

1. Open a web page.
2. If necessary, in the **INSERT** panel, from the drop-down list, select **Common.**
3. In the **INSERT** panel, click **Head** and select a head element.
   - Select **Meta** to insert information such as character encoding, author name, or copyright information.
   - Select **Keywords** to insert keywords for the web page, which can be accessed by search engines.
   - Select **Description** to insert a description of the page.
   - Select **Refresh** to set the browser to refresh the page automatically.
   - Select **Base** to specify the base URL for the document links.
   - Select **Link** to specify the relationship between the web page and any other file.
4. In the dialog box that is displayed, specify the attributes for the selected head element.
5. Save the web page.

Procedure Reference: Set the Page Properties

To set the page properties:

1. Display the **Page Properties** dialog box.
   - Choose **Modify→Page Properties** or;
   - In the **PROPERTIES** panel, click **Page Properties.**
2. In the **Page Properties** dialog box, in the **Category** list box, select the desired category.
3. Specify the desired properties for the page.
4. Click **OK** to apply the changes.

Procedure Reference: Insert a div Tag

To insert a <div> tag:

1. In the document window, place the insertion point at the desired position or select the desired text where you want to insert the <div> tag.
2. Display the **Insert Div Tag** dialog box.
   - Choose **Insert→Layout Objects→Div Tag** or;
   - In the **INSERT** panel, click **Insert Div Tag.**
3. From the **Insert** drop-down list, select the desired option.
4. If necessary, from the **Class** drop-down list, select the desired class style you want to apply.
5. If necessary, in the **ID** text box, type an ID.
6. If necessary, click **New CSS Rule** and create a CSS rule for the <div> tag.

7. Click **OK.**
8. If necessary, in the document window, within the `<div>` tag, type the desired content.

Procedure Reference: Preview a Web Page

To preview a web page:

1. Open the desired web page.
2. Preview the web page in the installed browser application.

    - Choose **File→Preview in Browser→<Installed Browser Application>** or;
    - On the **Document** toolbar, click the **Preview/Debug in Browser** button and choose **<Installed Browser Application>.**

ACTIVITY 3-2
Formatting Web Pages Using HTML Properties

Data Files:

index.html, clients.html

Before You Begin:

If the Our Global Company site was previously defined in Dreamweaver, you must modify the Local Root folder and Default images folder in the site definition so that it is based on the new data from the C:\084502Data\Designing Web Pages\Our Global Company folder.

Scenario:

You entered the required content on the web pages. While reviewing them, you find that there are unnecessary spaces between the paragraphs. In addition, you have a list of your clients and partners on the clients.html page, which does not appear well formatted. You want to have consistent formatting for the text.

---

1. Remove unnecessary spacing between paragraphs.

    a. In the **FILES** panel, expand the **Site - Our Global Company** folder.

    b. In the **FILES** panel, scroll down, and double-click **index.html.**

    c. On the **Document** toolbar, click **Code** to switch to Code view.

    d. Verify that there are empty paragraph tags, <p> </p>, between each paragraph.

    e. On the **Document** toolbar, click **Design** to switch to Design view.

    f. Click at the beginning of the text "Global Company" in the first paragraph and press **Backspace** to remove the extra space.

    g. Click at the beginning of the second paragraph and press **Backspace** two times to remove the extra space.

    h. Click at the beginning of the third paragraph and press **Backspace** two times to remove the extra space.

    i. Switch to Code view.

    j. Observe that the empty paragraph tags have been removed.

    k. On line **11,** click after the text "Welcome," hold down **Shift,** and click after the tag <br /> to select it.

    l. Press **Delete** to remove the line break.

    m. Switch to Design view.

    n. Choose **File→Save** to save the file.

---

2. Bold format the words "Clients" and "Partners."

    a.   In the **FILES** panel, double-click **clients.html.**

    b.   Below the text "Clients and Partners," double-click the word **"Clients"** to select it.

    c.   In the **PROPERTIES** panel, click **HTML,** `<> HTML` and then click the **Bold** button, `B` to apply bold formatting.

    d.   Below the text "IBooks Publishing Company," double-click the word **"Partners"** to select it.

    e.   In the **PROPERTIES** panel, click the **Bold** button to apply bold formatting.

3.   Format the Clients and Partners list.

    a.   Click before the text "ABC Book," hold down **Shift,** and click after the text "IBooks Publishing Company" to select the companies' names.

    b.   In the **PROPERTIES** panel, click the **Ordered List** button. `≔`

    c.   Scroll down, click before the text "QwikLearn Inc.," hold down **Shift,** and click after the text "e-KNOWledge Inc." to select the four companies' names.

    d.   In the **PROPERTIES** panel, click the **Unordered List** button. `≔`

    e.   Click in the document window to deselect the unordered list.

    f.   Choose **File→Save** to save the file.

4.   Preview the web page in a browser.

    a.   Choose **File→Preview in Browser→IExplore** to preview the web page in Internet Explorer.

    b.   Close the Internet Explorer window.

    c.   Choose **File→Close** to close the clients.html file.

ACTIVITY 3-3
Formatting a Web Page Using CSS

Data Files:

index.html

Before You Begin:

The index.html file is open.

Scenario:

You want to enhance the appearance of a page to make it more appealing. You need to ensure that all the paragraphs and headings have the same formatting and the content is organized properly.

---

1. Apply the heading format to the word "Welcome."

    a. In the document window, double-click the word **"Welcome."**

    b. In the **PROPERTIES** panel, from the **Format** drop-down list, select **Heading 1.**

2. Specify CSS properties to format the heading.

    a. In the **PROPERTIES** panel, click **Page Properties.**

    b. In the **Page Properties** dialog box, in the **Category** list box, select **Headings (CSS).**

    c. From the **Heading font** drop-down list, select **Arial, Helvetica, sans-serif.**

    d. In the **Heading 1** text box, click and type *20*

    e. In the second **Heading 1** drop-down list, verify that **px** is selected to ensure that the value is specified in pixels.

    f. In the color text box to the right of the **Heading 1** drop-down list, click and type *#999* to apply gray color to the heading.

    g. Click **OK** to apply the page properties.

    h. Click in the document window to deselect the text.

3. Create a CSS rule for the <p> tag.

    a. At the bottom of the **CSS STYLES** panel, click the **New CSS Rule** button.

    b. In the **New CSS Rule** dialog box, in the **Selector Type** section, from the drop-down list, select **Tag (redefines an HTML element).**

    c. In the **Selector Name** section, in the drop-down list, verify that **p** is selected.

    d. In the **Rule Definition** section, in the drop-down list, verify that **(This document only)** is selected.

    e. Click **OK.**

---

    f.   In the **CSS Rule definition for p** dialog box, from the **Font-family** drop-down list, select **Arial, Helvetica, sans-serif.**

    g.   From the **Font-size** drop-down list, select **12.**

    h.   In the **Color** text box, click and type *#000*

    i.   Click **OK** to add the CSS rule.

4.   Create a container for the main text.

    a.   Choose **Edit→Select All** to select all the text.

    b.   In the **FILES** panel group, select the **INSERT** panel.

    c.   In the **INSERT** panel, from the drop-down list, select **Common.**

    d.   Click **Insert Div Tag.**

    e.   In the **Insert Div Tag** dialog box, in the **Insert** drop-down list, verify that **Wrap around selection** is selected.

    f.   In the **ID** text box, click and type *main*

    g.   Click **OK.**

5.   Create an ID style for the container.

    a.   At the bottom of the **CSS STYLES** panel, click the **New CSS Rule** button.

    b.   In the **New CSS Rule** dialog box, in the **Selector Type** section, in the drop-down list, verify that **ID (applies to only one HTML element)** is selected, and in the **Selector Name** section, in the drop-down list, verify that **#main** is selected.

    c.   In the **Rule Definition** section, in the drop-down list, verify that **(This document only)** is selected and click **OK.**

    d.   In the **CSS Rule definition for #main** dialog box, in the **Category** list box, select **Box.**

    e.   In the **Width** text box, click and type *540*

    f.   From the **Float** drop-down list, select **left.**

    g.   In the **Padding** section, verify that the **Same for all** check box is checked.

    h.   In the **Top** text box, click and type *5*

    i.   Click **OK** to add the CSS rule.

6.   Preview the web page in a browser.

    a.   Choose **File→Save.**

    b.   Choose **File→Preview in Browser→IExplore** to preview the web page in Internet Explorer.

    c.   Close the Internet Explorer window.

    d.   Close the index.html file.

TOPIC C
Identify Copyright and Citation Requirements

You formatted the text on a web page and are now ready to add more content to the pages of a site. Before doing so, you need to know the content rights of other content authors and protect the online information you provide on a site. In this topic, you will identify copyright and citation requirements.

With the vast wealth of information available on the Internet, it is easy to forget that not all information is free for the taking. Unlike opening the first page of a book and seeing the printed copyright text, it is not always clearly evident whether online content is protected with a copyright. To further complicate things, it has become an all-too-common practice to download whatever content we want, irrespective of whether it may or may not be legal. Keeping up-to-date on copyright and citation requirements not only protects your own information, but also acts as a reminder to respect that of others.

Copyright Terminologies

A copyright protects the works of individuals for a set period of time. When presenting content on the web, it is important to understand and use copyright terms correctly.

Term	Description
Copyright	Enacted by Congress to protect the writings of authors. A copyright gives the owner exclusive right to reproduce, distribute, perform, or display their work.
Copyrightable work	Any work for which a copyright can be obtained is a copyrightable work. Copyrightable works are generally classified into various categories. They are given below: • Literary works such as books, manuscripts, and computer programs. • Pictorial works such as graphic art, photographs, and technical drawings. • Musical works (including Drama) such as composition and lyrics, screenplays, and motion pictures. • Sound recordings such as music, audio (spoken) works, and sound effects.
Derivative work	Work based upon a copyrighted work such as an update, revision, or adaptation.

Term	Description
Duration	The length of time a work can be copyrighted. By default, the length of time is the life of the copyright owner plus 50 or 70 years. There are variations based on factors such as whether the work has been published or if both an individual and a company originated the copyright.
Fair use doctrine	Traditionally applied to academic use. For example: making and distributing copies of copyrighted works for teaching purposes.
Infringement	The unauthorized use of copyrighted work that violates any or all of the copyright owner's rights.
Intellectual property	Property from original thought/original creative work that is protected by law.

Copyright Permission

To use copyrighted work on the pages of a website, you need to obtain written permission from the copyright holder. A permission request must include the purpose, duration, and a description of how the material will be used. If you plan to create a link to another site, notify the administrator of that site. While seeking permission, if a copyright holder cannot be located, you will not be able to use the work.

Locating Copyright Holders

Some of the sources you may use to locate the copyright holder from whom you want to secure permission include:

- Publisher of the work
- Webmaster of a website
- Photographer
- University or academic institution
- Researcher
- Business organization

The Copyright Notice

When displaying a particular website's content for which you have copyrights, you need to indicate that the content is protected by a copyright. A statement indicating copyright ownership that includes the owner's name and the year the copyright was acquired is ample proof of copyright protection. However, the most visual and dependable way to show copyright ownership is a copyright notice. Often attached to a copyrighted work, the copyright notice includes:

- The word "Copyright"
- The copyright symbol ©
- The copyright holder's name
- The phrase "All Rights Reserved"

Citing Internet Content

The web is particularly vulnerable to copyright infringement, especially when a copyright notice is not available. It is, however, important to cite any content you copy from the web. The format to use for web content citations is specific to the type of content.

Content Type	Citation
Audio	Description or title of sound in the http://address/ filename format, and date of audio file.
	If the date is not available, use the date of your download.
Image	Description or title of the image in the http:// address/filename format, and date of the material.
	If the date is not available, use the date of your download.
Video clip	Description or title of the video clip in the http:// address/filename format, and date of the material.
	If the date is not available, use the date of your download.
World Wide Web	Author or title of the item in the http://address/ filename format, and date of the material.
	If the date is not available, use the date of your download.

Academic Standards

Scholars who publish material within an academic institution must adhere to higher standards—crediting the originator of any quoted material, even when just paraphrasing another's ideas. You cannot paraphrase what someone else says without giving credit to the originator.

Unauthorized Music and Video Downloads

Unauthorized reproduction and distribution of electronic and audio-visual media falls under the heading of piracy. While it is lawful to download some music, laws regarding the sharing and downloading of music vary from country to country. The U.S. Digital Millennium Copyright Act deems unauthorized copying of copyrighted music as illegal. Infringement of online copyrighted music is punishable by up to three years in prison and $250,000 in fine.

ACTIVITY 3-4
Reviewing Copyright and Citation Principles

Scenario:

Once you are proficient in Dreamweaver, you will work with web pages of many sites. During the development of the pages, it can be easy to forget the legalities imposed on original and copied material. To ensure that you have a solid understanding of copyright and citation principles, you want to test your knowledge.

1. **Which term describes the illegal use of a copyrighted work?**

   a) Fair use doctrine

   b) Copyrightable work

   c) Infringement

   d) Derivative work

2. **Which elements will you use as part of a copyright notice? (Choose three.)**

   a) The copyright symbol (©).

   b) The country of the copyright registration.

   c) The word "copyright."

   d) The phrase "All Rights Reserved."

TOPIC D
Insert Images

You created and formatted a web page. Now, you may want to make it look more attractive. In this topic, you will insert images.

A web page that contains only textual content might not interest a user. By adding images, you can make the web page visually appealing. It will also illustrate the site's content clearly to the user.

Graphic File Formats for the Web

There are three graphic file formats that are commonly used on web pages. The following table describes these formats.

File format	Description
Graphic Interchange Format (GIF)	Uses a maximum of 256 colors and therefore is most useful for images with few colors or with large areas of flat colors. You can reduce the file size of GIF images by reducing the number of colors within the image. GIF images also support transparency, so page background can be made visible through portions of the image. However, they only support single color transparency.
Joint Photographic Experts Group (JPEG)	Uses compression to dramatically reduce the file size, thus allowing for faster download and display. When the compression level in a JPEG image is increased, the file size and quality are reduced. JPEG images use *lossy compression* methods, resulting in pixel information being lost to reduce overall file size. JPEG images are best suited for photographs and other images that contain more than 256 colors. JPEG images do not support transparency, so the background of your image should match that of the web page to avoid a visible rectangular area around the image when viewed.

File format	Description
Portable Network Graphic (PNG)	Supports background transparency and *lossless compression*. PNG does not reduce the image size like JPEG does. There are three types of PNG formats.
	• PNG-8 supports 256 colors and single color transparency. File compression is better than GIF, resulting in smaller file sizes.
	• PNG-24 supports millions of colors and multi-level transparency. File compression is lossless and file sizes are comparable with JPEG.
	• PNG-32 supports not only millions of colors but also alpha transparency. File compression is lossless, resulting in better images than JPEG, but with a larger file size.

Web-Safe Colors

Web-safe colors are 216 colors that are used while most computer monitors are capable of displaying only 256 colors. Modern PCs can display millions of colors, making use of web-safe colors as a choice and not a necessity. Every color in the web-safe palette can be specified by an RGB value, where each component, R, G, and B, is represented by 0, 51, 102, 153, 204, or 255. While designing web pages, it is best practice to use colors that fall within these 216 colors. It is also advisable to optimize images to contain only web-safe colors.

Built-In Web-Safe Palettes

Most professional web design programs, such as Adobe Dreamweaver CS5, have a built-in web-safe palette. In Dreamweaver, the **Color Cubes** and **Continuous Tone** palettes display 216 web-safe colors.

Integration with Adobe Fireworks CS5

Adobe® Fireworks® CS5 is extensively used to prepare images for web pages. When an image is exported from Fireworks to the root folder of a site defined in Dreamweaver, the information about the source file is stored in the site. If the image need be edited, the source file can be opened in Fireworks directly from Dreamweaver.

Image Properties

Image properties allow you to control how images are displayed on a web page. Some of the common image properties include width, height, spacing, alignment, and alternate text.

Property	Allows You To
Width and Height	Control the display size of an image. This does not change the actual size of the image.
Vertical and Horizontal space	Add space vertically or horizontally around an image by specifying values in pixels. These properties are deprecated in XHTML.
Alignment	Set the alignment of an image in relation to text within a paragraph.

Property	Allows You To
Alternate Text	Display an alternate text label if the web browser is not set to display an image.
Image Source	Change the image by specifying its location.
Border	Add a border for the image. The width of the border is specified in pixels.

Use of Alternate Text

If an HTML page contains images, the text on the page gets downloaded before the images do. Placeholders indicating the presence of an image appear on the page while images are loading. Placeholders also appear if the viewer has turned off the option of automatic image loading; this option is turned off when the connection is very slow. In such instances, the alternate text that appears in the image placeholder gives a description of the image. It also appears when you move the mouse pointer over an image, but only certain browsers support it.

Alternate text is also used to ensure that the website complies with Section 508 for accessibility standards and the WCAG Priority 1 checklist. When the page is accessed, screen readers will read the alternate text specified for the image. This is very helpful for visually impaired people who use screen readers.

Working with Images in Dreamweaver

Dreamweaver provides options to insert and set properties to display images on a web page. However, Dreamweaver does not provide options to edit and save images. Other image-editing applications need to be used to edit, optimize, and save images in a suitable format. Image manipulation in Dreamweaver is restricted to setting properties that affect the display of images on a web page. The **PROPERTIES** panel also has options to crop images, adjust the brightness and contrast of an image, and sharpen images. Though the original image file is not altered, the appearance of the image on the web page changes.

Alignment Options

The **Align** drop-down list in the **PROPERTIES** panel provides several alignment options for aligning images on a web page. Some of the commonly used options are top, middle, bottom, left, and right alignment.

The following table describes the alignment options used in XHTML.

Alignment Option	Description
Top	The top of the image is aligned with the top of the tallest object in the current line.
Middle	The middle of the image is aligned with the baseline of the current line.
Bottom	The bottom of the image is aligned with the baseline of the text in the current line.
Left or **Right**	The image is aligned to the left or right edge of the browser window or table cell, and the text in the current line flows around the left or right side of the image.

CSS Image Properties

CSS image properties are defined as CSS rules that affect the appearance of images on a web page. They are chiefly categorized as **Background, Box,** and **Positioning.**

Category	Description
Background	Contains properties to define background settings such as the background image, background color, repetition of the image in the background, and positioning of the image.
Box	Contains properties, such as the width, height, margin between the image and surrounding elements, padding between the image and its border, and appearance of the image with respect to other elements on the page, to define the placement of images on a page.
Positioning	Contains properties, such as the positioning method, visibility, stacking order, and behavior of the image container, to define the positioning of an image.

How to Insert Images

Procedure Reference: Insert an Image on a Page

To insert an image on a page:

1. Click in the desired location to place the insertion point.
2. Display the **Select Image Source** dialog box.
   - Choose **Insert→Image** or;
   - In the **INSERT** panel, click the **Images** drop-down arrow and select **Image.**
3. Navigate to the desired folder, select a file, and click **OK.**
4. In the **Image Tag Accessibility Attributes** dialog box, in the **Alternate text** text box, type an alternate name for the image and click **OK.**

Procedure Reference: Edit an Image in Fireworks

To edit an image in Fireworks:

1. Open a web page with an image exported from Adobe® Fireworks® CS5.
2. If necessary, display the **PROPERTIES** panel.
3. In the document window, select the image.
4. Open the image in Fireworks.
   - Right-click the image and choose **Edit With Fireworks** or;
   - In the **PROPERTIES** panel, click **Edit.**
5. Edit the image in Fireworks.
6. In Fireworks, click **Done** to update the image in Dreamweaver.
7. If necessary, preview the web page.

Procedure Reference: Set Image Properties

To set image properties:

1. Select the image.
2. In the **PROPERTIES** panel, set the desired image properties.

Procedure Reference: Scale an Image

To scale an image:

1. Open a web page.
2. If necessary, insert an image.
3. In the document window, select the image.
4. Resize the image in the document window.
   - Drag the selection handle on the right of the image, to set its width.
   - Drag the selection handle below the image, to set its height.
   - Drag the selection handle at the bottom-right corner of the image, to set its width and height simultaneously.
   - Hold down **Shift** and drag the selection handle at the bottom-right corner of the image, to set its width and height simultaneously and maintain the proportion of the width to the height.
5. If necessary, in the **PROPERTIES** panel, specify values in the **W** and **H** text boxes to set the dimensions of the image accurately.
6. If necessary, in the **PROPERTIES** panel, click the **Reset Size** button to reset the image to its original size.
7. Save the file.
8. If necessary, preview the web page.

ACTIVITY 3-5
Inserting Images

Data Files:

index.html, banner_head.jpg, home_up.gif, ourcompany_up.gif, news_up.gif, clients_up.gif, career_up.gif

Before You Begin:

1. In the C:\084502Data\Designing Web Pages\Our Global Company folder, rename the index.html file as index_old.html.

2. Copy the index.html file in the C:\084502Data\Designing Web Pages folder to the C:\084502Data\Designing Web Pages\Our Global Company folder.

Scenario:

You have images to add to the website to complement the information on the home page. You also have a banner image for the site and some images for navigation purposes.

---

1. Add the image in the banner_head.jpg file to the page.

    a. In the **FILES** panel, double-click **index.html.**

    b. Click in the first container for the header and choose **Insert→Image.**

    c. In the **Select Image Source** dialog box, double-click the **images** folder.

    d. Select **banner_head.jpg** and click **OK.**

    e. In the **Image Tag Accessibility Attributes** dialog box, in the **Alternate text** text box, type *Our Global Company* and click **OK.**

---

2. Add images to the navigation menu.

    a. Press the **Right Arrow** key two times to place the insertion point in the container below the header container.

    b. Choose **Insert→Image.**

    c. If necessary, in the **Select Image Source** dialog box, navigate to the C:\084502Data\Designing Web Pages\Our Global Company\images folder.

    d. In the **Select Image Source** dialog box, select **home_up.gif,** and then click **OK.**

    e. In the **Image Tag Accessibility Attributes** dialog box, in the **Alternate text** text box, type *Home* and click **OK.**

    f. Choose **Insert→Image.**

    g. In the **Select Image Source** dialog box, scroll to the right, select **ourcompany_up.gif,** and click **OK.**

    h. In the **Image Tag Accessibility Attributes** dialog box, in the **Alternate text** text box, type *Our Company* and click **OK.**

    i. Similarly, insert images and set their alternate text as follows:

- **news_up** with text as *News*
- **clients_up** with text as **Clients**
- **career_up** with text as *Career*

j. Choose **File→Save.**

k. Close the index.html file.

TOPIC E

Insert Tables

You inserted images on a web page. Now, you may need to present content in an organized way. In this topic, you will insert tables.

It is often necessary to display tabular information on web pages to present data in a structured and organized manner. By using tables, you will be able to present data in a tabular format.

Tables

Definition:

A *table* is a container that enables you to organize text or graphics. Tables consist of boxes called cells. A group of cells arranged vertically is called a column and a group of cells arranged horizontally is called a row. A table may have numerous rows and columns to accommodate data. Individual cells in a table can be modified by adding margins, borders, and colors.

Example:

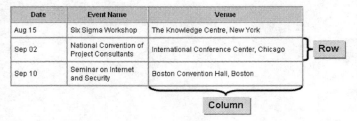

Figure 3-6: A table on a web page.

The <table> Tag

The <table> tag is used to create tables. The table structure is defined by using the <tr> tags within the <table> tag to define rows in a table and the <td> tags within the <tr> tag to define individual cells in a row. The table tag can contain other tags that define the structure of the table. The following table describes the tags that can be used within the table tag.

Tag	Description
<tr>	Used to define table rows. A table tag can contain multiple <tr> tags.
<td>	Used to define table cells within a row. Each <tr> tag can contain multiple <td> tags.
<th>	Used instead of <td> to define a cell as a header cell. The text within the <th> tag will appear centered and in bold format.
<thead>	Used to identify a row or a group of rows as the table header. It must contain at least one <tr> tag.

Tag	Description
`<tbody>`	Used to identify a row or a group of rows as the table body. It must contain at least one `<tr>` tag.
`<tfoot>`	Used to identify a row or a group of rows as the table footer. It must contain at least one `<tr>` tag.
`<colgroup>`	Used to specify attributes that help group columns for formatting.
`<col>`	Used to specify attributes for individual columns in a table or in a `colgroup` tag.

Nested Tables

Nested tables are tables placed within a table cell. They allow you to create a complex design grid that will help in the alignment of text and graphics. You can use as many nesting levels as you need to create the grid you want. Nested tables result in complex HTML code. CSS is now favored over nested tables to layout page content.

The Table Dialog Box

The **Table** dialog box provides several options that enable you to specify the attributes of a table while creating it.

The following table describes the options in the dialog box.

Option	Used To
Rows and **Columns**	Specify the number of rows and columns to be created in a table.
Table width	Specify the width of a table, either in pixels or as a percentage. When specified in pixels, the table width is a fixed value, but when specified as a percentage, the table width is relative to the size of the browser window.
Border thickness	Place a visible border between table cells and around table edges, and specify the thickness of the border. The larger the number, the thicker the border is. If you do not want visible borders, enter zero in this text box.
Cell padding	Control the distance between the edge of a cell and its content. If you do not want any cell padding, enter the value as zero. Leaving it blank will add a default amount of space.
Cell spacing	Specify the amount of spacing between table cells. If you do not want any cell spacing, enter the value as zero. Leaving it blank will add a default amount of spacing.

Option	Used To
Header	Insert a header row for the table. The content in the header row is centered and appears bold. You can designate the top, left, or both portions of the table as the header row. If you do not want a header, select the **None** option.
Caption	Insert a caption for the table.
Summary	Give a summary of the table. You can use this option to enter a brief description about the contents of the table. This will be useful for users who need the aid of screen readers.

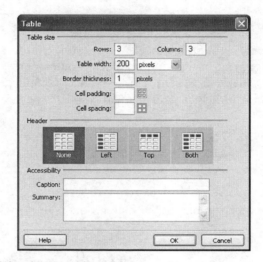

Figure 3-7: *The Table dialog box and its options.*

Table Properties

The **PROPERTIES** panel allows you to modify the table attributes to control the appearance of a table. In addition to the properties available in the **Table** dialog box, you can also specify the alignment of the table relative to other elements on the page.

The Table Widths Visual Aid

When you select a table or place the insertion point in a table in Design view, the table width and column width are displayed in the **Table Widths** visual aid at the top or bottom of the table. These values of width are expressed in pixels, percentage, or both. The column header menu, available in the visual aid, provides options to clear and adjust the width and also insert columns. This visual aid is available in both **Standard** and **Expanded** table modes.

Table Width

The width of tables can be set using one of two methods. Width can be specified as a percentage value of the page width, or it can be set in pixel values. Dreamweaver allows you to set the width of tables using any of these methods while creating a table. Table sizes can also be modified later using the **PROPERTIES** panel. Tables can be resized in the document window by first selecting a table and then dragging the handles on its border.

CSS Table Properties

CSS table properties are defined as CSS rules that affect the appearance of tables on a web page. They are categorized as **Box, Border,** and **Type.**

Category	Description
Box	Contains properties, such as the width, height, margin between the table and surrounding elements, padding between the table and its border, and appearance of tables with respect to other elements, to define the placement of tables on a page.
Border	Contains properties such as the border style, width, and color that define the appearance of borders around the table.
Type	Contains properties such as the font family, font size, color, font style, and text and font characteristics that define the attributes of text used in tables.

CSS Properties

CSS properties organized under various categories in the **CSS Rule Definition** dialog box can be used to set properties for various elements on a web page such as text, images, and tables. Some of these properties will be applicable to more than one element. When you create a CSS rule, you can set multiple properties that can be applied to various elements.

Graphics in Table Cells

Just as you can select background colors for tables and individual cells, you can place images in the background of table cells. Background images automatically get tiled within the cell irrespective of how tall or wide the cell becomes when the image is placed in it. You can specify the background image for a table cell using the background image property for a CSS rule.

Table Modes

You can create and modify tables using one of two modes. The following table describes the table modes.

Table Mode	Description
Standard	Tables are presented as a grid of rows and columns. This is the default mode in Adobe Dreamweaver CS5.
Expanded	Tables are presented with temporarily added extra cell spacing, padding, and borders for easy editing. While creating nested tables, this option will clearly define where a table begins and where it ends, thereby allowing you to add text and images to individual cells easily.

How to Insert Tables

Procedure Reference: Insert a Table

To insert a table:

1. Place the insertion point at the desired location on the web page.

2. Display the **Table** dialog box.

    - In the **INSERT** panel, click the **Table** button or;

    - Choose **Insert→Table.**

3. Specify the desired settings and click **OK.**

4. If necessary, in the **INSERT** panel, click **Layout** and then select **Expanded** to work in the expanded mode.

5. Add content to the table.

    - Click in a cell and type the text or add an image.

    - Copy and paste the content.

        a. Copy the desired content.

        b. Click in the desired cell.

        c. Choose **Edit→Paste.**

6. If necessary, select the desired region in the table and add a row or column.

    - Right-click the selected row or column, choose **Table,** and then choose the desired command to insert a row or column.

    - Choose **Insert→Table Objects** and then choose the desired command or;

    - Choose **Modify→Table** and then choose the desired command.

7. If necessary, select the desired region in the table and delete a row or column.

    - Right-click the selected row or column, choose **Table,** and then choose the desired command to delete a row or column or;

    - Choose **Modify→Table** and then choose a command to delete a row or column.

 When you are in the last cell of the table, you can press **Tab** to add a new row.

8. If necessary, create a CSS rule for the table.

Table Selection Methods

You can select a particular cell, row, or a column in a table to apply formatting to it. There are a number of methods to select a region in a table.

- Place the mouse pointer on the left border of the desired row. When the mouse pointer changes to a right arrow, click to select the row.

- Place the mouse pointer on the top border of the desired column. When the mouse pointer changes to a down arrow, click to select the column.

- Click and drag to select multiple cells.

- Click a cell, hold down **Shift,** and click another cell to select all the cells between the two cells.

- Click in a cell to select it.

The Paste Special Dialog Box

The **Paste Special** dialog box allows you to determine the formatting options for the text pasted into Dreamweaver CS5.

It consists of four options:

- **Text only:** Allows you to paste unformatted text. All formatting in the original text, including line breaks and paragraphs, is removed.

- **Text with structure:** Allows you to retain the basic structure of the original text, but removes all formatting. You can retain options such as paragraph structures, tables, and lists, but formatting such as bold and italics will not be retained.

- **Text with structure plus basic formatting:** Allows you to retain both structured and simple HTML formats from the original text.

- **Text with structure plus full formatting:** Allows you to retain all structures, HTML formatting, and CSS styles from the original text.

Procedure Reference: Edit Table Properties

To edit table properties:

1. Select a table.
2. In the **PROPERTIES** panel, edit the table properties.
   - In the **Rows** text box, type a value to change the number of rows in the table.
   - In the **Cols** text box, type a value to change the number of columns in the table.
   - In the **CellPad** text box, type a value to change cell padding.
   - In the **CellSpace** text box, type a value to change cell spacing.

Procedure Reference: Format a Table

To format a table:

1. Select the desired region of the table.
2. Format the table using the **PROPERTIES** panel.
   - In the **PROPERTIES** panel, click the **Merges selected cells using spans** button to merge the selected cells.

 You can merge only the adjacent cells in the table. You can also merge the cells in an entire row or column.

   - Split a cell.
     a. In the **PROPERTIES** panel, click the **Splits cell into rows or columns** button to split a selected cell.
     b. In the **Split Cell** dialog box, specify the options to split a cell into rows or columns and click **OK.**
   - In the **W** text box, click and type a value to change the width, and in the **H** text box, click and type a value to change the height.
   - Select the table and from the **Align** drop-down list, select the desired option to align the table.
   - Insert a background graphic into the table.

a. Select the entire table.

b. In the **PROPERTIES** panel, to the right of the **Bg** text box, click the **Background URL of cell** button.

c. In the **Select Image Source** dialog box, navigate to the desired folder, select the file, and click **OK.**

● Add a background color to the cells.

■ In the second **Bg** text box, click and type the hexadecimal value of a color or;

■ To the left of the **Bg** text box, click the color swatch button and select the desired color.

Procedure Reference: Create a Nested Table

To create a nested table:

1. Click in a table cell.
2. Display the **Table** dialog box.
3. Specify settings in the **Table** dialog box and click **OK.**
4. Add content to the table.

Procedure Reference: Apply Class Styles to a Web Page

To apply class styles to a web page:

1. In the document window, select the desired content.
2. Apply the desired style to the selected text.

● In the **PROPERTIES** panel, click **CSS** and from the **Targeted Rule** drop-down list, select the desired class style.

● In the **CSS STYLES** panel, right-click the desired class style and choose **Apply.**

● In the **CSS STYLES** panel, select the desired style and from the **Options** menu, choose **Apply** or;

● Choose **Format→CSS Styles** and then choose the desired style.

3. Save the web page.

ACTIVITY 3-6
Creating a Table

Data Files:

contactus.html, Contact Info.txt

Before You Begin:

1. Navigate to the C:\084502Data\Designing Web Pages\Our Global Company folder and open the Contact Info.txt file in Notepad.
2. Switch to the Dreamweaver application.

Scenario:

Your site visitors may want to contact or reach your office for details and queries about the services provided by your company. You need to include the contact details of the various branches of Our Global Company, Inc., located worldwide, on the Contact Us page. You also need to ensure that the information is presented in an organized way.

---

1. Create a table.

    a. In the **FILES** panel, double-click **contactus.html.**

    b. Click at the end of the text "Corporate offices:" and press **Enter.**

    c. In the **INSERT** panel, click **Table.**

    d. In the **Table** dialog box, in the **Table size** section, in the **Rows** text box, type *10* and press **Tab.**

    e. In the **Columns** text box, type *2* and press **Tab.**

    f. In the **Table width** text box, type *500* and press **Tab** two times.

    g. In the **Border thickness** text box, type *0* and press **Tab.**

    h. In the **Cell padding** text box, type *10* and press **Tab.**

    i. In the **Cell spacing** text box, type *0*

    j. Click **OK** to create the table.

---

2. Add content to the table.

    a. In the first row, click in the first cell, type *Location* and then press **Tab.**

    b. Type *Address* and press **Tab.**

    c. Switch to the Notepad application.

    d. On the second line, click and drag over the text "New York," to select it.

    e. Choose **Edit→Copy.**

    f. Switch to the Dreamweaver application.

    g. In the second row, click in the first cell and choose **Edit→Paste.**

h.   Switch to the Notepad application.

i.   On the third line, click before the text "1177 ABC Avenue," hold down **Shift,** and on the seventh line, click after the text "Facsimile: 212–555–1111."

j.   Choose **Edit→Copy.**

k.   Switch to the Dreamweaver application.

l.   In the second row, click in the second cell and choose **Edit→Paste.**

3.   Add the remaining addresses.

a.   Similarly, copy the remaining contact details from the Contact Info.txt file and paste them in the respective cells.

b.   Choose **File→Save.**

c.   Close the Contact Info.txt file

Do not close the contactus.html file, because it is necessary to perform the next activity.

ACTIVITY 3-7
Formatting a Table

Data Files:

contactus.html

Before You Begin:

Scroll to the top of the page.

Scenario:

Because the table content on a page appears to be similar, it makes reading difficult. Therefore, you decide to enhance the appearance of the table so that the content in the table can be easily distinguished.

---

1. Create a CSS rule for the table header.

    a. At the bottom of the **CSS STYLES** panel, click the **New CSS Rule** button.

    b. In the **New CSS Rule** dialog box, in the **Selector Type** section, from the drop-down list, select **Class (can apply to any HTML element).**

    c. In the **Selector Name** section, in the first text box, click and type *.thead*

    d. In the **Rule Definition** section, in the drop-down list, verify that **(This document only)** is selected and click **OK.**

---

2. Specify CSS properties for the thead class style.

    a. In the **CSS Rule definition for .thead** dialog box, from the **Font-size** drop-down list, select **14.**

    b. From the **Font-weight** drop-down list, select **bolder.**

    c. In the **Category** list box, select **Background.**

    d. In the **Background-color** text box, click and type *#B6D9EF*

    e. In the **Category** list box, select **Block.**

    f. From the **Text-align** drop-down list, select **center.**

    g. In the **Category** list box, select **Box.**

    h. In the **Height** text box, click and type *20*

    i. Click **OK** to add the CSS rule.

---

3. Create a CSS rule for the table row color.

    a. At the bottom of the **CSS STYLES** panel, click the **New CSS Rule** button.

    b. In the **New CSS Rule** dialog box, in the **Selector Type** section, in the drop-down list, verify that **Class (can apply to any HTML element)** is selected.

---

   c.   In the **Selector Name** section, in the first text box, type *.trcolor*

   d.   In the **Rule Definition** section, in the drop-down list, verify that **(This document only)** is selected and click **OK.**

   e.   In the **CSS Rule definition for .trcolor** dialog box, in the **Category** list box, select **Background.**

   f.   In the **Background-color** text box, click and type *#E9E9E9*

   g.   Click **OK** to add the CSS rule.

4.   Align the table to the center.

   a.   Click in the table and choose **Modify→Table→Select Table** to select it.

   b.   In the **PROPERTIES** panel, from the **Align** drop-down list, select **Center.**

5.   Apply class styles to the table.

   a.   Place the mouse pointer on the left border of the first row. When the mouse pointer changes to a right arrow, click to select the first row.

   b.   In the **PROPERTIES** panel, click **CSS.**

   c.   From the **Targeted Rule** drop-down list, select **thead.**

   d.   Observe that the class style is applied to the header row.

   e.   Scroll down and select the row that contains the contact details of San Francisco.

   f.   In the **PROPERTIES** panel, from the **Targeted Rule** drop-down list, select **trcolor.**

   g.   Similarly, apply the trcolor class style to the rows that contain contact details of Boston, Toronto, and London.

6.   Preview the web page in a browser.

   a.   Choose **File→Save.**

   b.   Choose **File→Preview in Browser→IExplore** to preview the web page in Internet Explorer.

   c.   Maximize the Internet Explorer window.

   d.   Scroll down to view the table.

   e.   Close the Internet Explorer window.

   f.   Close the contactus.html file.

TOPIC F
Import Data from Other Applications

You created a web page with content in the form of text, images, and tables. There may be times when you need to display the contents of a Microsoft® Word® document or a Microsoft® Excel® document. In this topic, you will import Word and Excel documents into your web page.

Sometimes, you may find that the content required for the web page is already available in a document that was created using a different application. Recreating this content in Dreamweaver can be a tiresome and time-consuming process. You can simplify the task by importing data from other applications into Dreamweaver.

Import Commands

Dreamweaver provides various commands to import external data into a web page. The import commands available in Dreamweaver are **XML into Template, Tabular Data, Word Document,** and **Excel Document.**

Import Command	Used To
XML into Template	Import data stored in an XML file into a document created based on the XML template.
Tabular Data	Import data available in a delimited text format such as a tab or a comma delimited file.
Word Document	Import content from Word documents.
Excel Document	Import data from Excel worksheets.

The Clean Up Word HTML Command

The **Clean Up Word HTML** command can be used to remove unwanted code that gets generated when you create or save an HTML file using Microsoft Word. You can clean up the HTML file by specifying the settings for the version of the Word document used, removing Word markup tags, cleaning up CSS and font tags, fixing invalidly nested tags, and applying source formatting. You can also choose to show a log of the process on completion.

How to Import Data from Other Applications

Procedure Reference: Import Word Documents into Dreamweaver

To import Word documents into Dreamweaver:

1. Open the desired web page and position the insertion point at the desired location.
2. Import a Word document.
    *   Import the document using the **File** menu.
        a. Choose **File→Import→Word Document.**
        b. In the **Import Word Document** dialog box, navigate to and select the desired document and then click **Open** or;
    *   Import the document using the **FILES** panel.
        a. From the **FILES** panel, click and drag the Word document to the document window.
        b. In the **Insert Document** dialog box, select the desired option.
            *   Select **Insert the contents** and then select the desired option to copy the formatting.
            *   Select **Create a link** to create a link to the Word document.
        c. Click **OK.**
3. If necessary, preview the web page in a browser.

Options Available to Import Content from Word Documents

When importing content from Word documents, a formatting option can be selected to specify how the content is to be formatted. The options available are as follows:

*   **Text only:** To import the text without any formatting applied to it.
*   **Text with structure (paragraphs, lists, tables):** To import text and display it on the web page with the same structure as in the Word document.
*   **Text, structure, basic formatting (bold, italic):** To import text and display it on the web page with the same structure as in the Word document and with bold and italic formatting retained.
*   **Text, structure, full formatting (bold, italic, styles):** To import text and display it on the web page with the same structure as in the Word document and with bold and italic formatting retained. Text styles defined in Word documents are also imported and applied to text.

Procedure Reference: Clean up the Word HTML Document

To clean up the Word HTML document:

1. Open the desired HTML web page created using Microsoft Word.
2. Choose **Commands→Clean Up Word HTML** to display the **Clean Up Word HTML** dialog box.
3. On the **Basic** tab, from the **Clean up HTML from** drop-down list, select the desired option.
4. Check or uncheck the desired check boxes to specify options to clean up the HTML.
5. If necessary, select the **Detailed** tab and check or uncheck the desired check boxes to specify options for removing Word-specific markup and cleaning up CSS.
6. Click **OK.**

Procedure Reference: Import Excel Worksheets into Dreamweaver

To import Excel worksheets into Dreamweaver:

1. Open the desired web page and position the insertion point at the desired location.

2. Import an Excel worksheet onto a web page.

   - Import the worksheet using the **File** menu.

     a. Choose **File→Import→Excel Document.**

     b. In the **Import Excel Document** dialog box, navigate to and select the desired worksheet and then click **Open** or;

   - Import the worksheet using the **FILES** panel.

     a. From the **FILES** panel, click and drag the Excel worksheet into the document window.

     b. In the **Insert Document** dialog box, select an option and click **OK.**

3. If necessary, preview the web page in a browser.

Procedure Reference: Import Tabular Data

To import tabular data:

1. If necessary, create a web page.

2. Open a web page and position the insertion point at the desired location.

3. Import tabular data onto a web page.

   a. Choose **File→Import→Tabular Data** to display the **Import Tabular Data** dialog box.

   b. Specify the data file.

      - In the **Data file** text box, type the name of the file to be imported.

      - To the right of the **Data file** text box, click **Browse** and select a data file.

   c. Specify the delimiting character.

      - From the **Delimiter** drop-down list, select a character to be used as the delimiting character.

      - To the right of the **Delimiter** drop-down list, in the text box, type a character to be used as the delimiting character.

   d. In the **Table width** section, select an option to specify the width of the table that will display the imported data.

      - Select the **Fit to data** option to create a table with column widths based on the imported data.

      - Specify the width of the table.

        ■ Select the **Set to** option.

        ■ In the text box to the right of the **Set to** option, type a value for the width of the table.

- From the drop-down list to the right of the text box, select the unit of measurement for the table width.

   e. If necessary, in the **Cell padding** text box, type a value for the cell padding of table cells.

   f. If necessary, in the **Cell spacing** text box, type a value for the cell spacing of table cells.

   g. From the **Format top row** drop-down list, specify the formatting for the top row of the table.

   - Select **No formatting** to display the content of the top row without any formatting.

   - Select **Bold** to display the content of the top row in bold format.

   - Select **Italic** to display the content of the top row in italics.

   - Select **Bold Italic** to display the content of the top row in italics and bold format.

   h. If necessary, in the **Border** text box, type a value for the width of the table border.

   i. Click **OK.**

4. If necessary, preview the web page in a browser.

ACTIVITY 3-8
Importing Word Documents into Dreamweaver

Data Files:

newsandevents.html, trademarks.html, News and Events.doc

Scenario:

One of your colleagues has given you a Word document with content that needs to be included in the News and Events page. Additionally, he has also provided the Trademarks and Copyrights page, which was saved as an HTML file using Microsoft Word. You need to ensure that content is available as HTML pages and do not contain any Word-specific markup tags.

1. Import the Word document into the web page.

   a. In the **FILES** panel, scroll down, and double-click **newsandevents.html.**

   b. In the document window, place the insertion point below the **Home** image.

   c. Choose **File→Import→Word Document.**

   d. In the **Import Word Document** dialog box, navigate to the C:\084502Data\Designing Web Pages\Our Global Company folder.

   e. Select **News and Events.doc** and click **Open.**

   f. Observe that the content of the Word document is imported onto the web page.

2. Preview the web page in a browser.

   a. Choose **File→Save.**

   b. Choose **File→Preview in Browser→IExplore** to preview the web page in Internet Explorer.

   c. Close the Internet Explorer window.

   d. Close the newsandevents.html file.

3. Clean up the Word HTML file.

   a. In the **FILES** panel, double-click **trademarks.html.**

   b. Switch to Code view.

   c. In the document window, scroll to the bottom of the code.

   d. Observe that there are 593 lines of code with some unnecessary tags in the HTML code.

   e. Choose **Commands→Clean Up Word HTML** to display the **Clean Up Word HTML** dialog box.

   f. In the **Clean up HTML from** drop-down list, verify that **Word 2000 and newer** is selected.

g.   Verify that all the check boxes are checked.

h.   Click **OK** to clean up the HTML file.

i.   In the **Dreamweaver** message box, observe the results and click **OK.**

j.   Scroll down to the bottom of the file.

k.   Observe that the number of lines of code is reduced to 89 and all the unnecessary tags are removed from the HTML code.

l.   Save the file.

m.   Close the trademarks.html file.

ACTIVITY 3-9
Importing Excel Worksheets into Dreamweaver

Data Files:

career.html, Email IDs.xls

Before You Begin:

1. In the **FILES** panel, double-click **career.html** to open it.
2. Switch to Design view.

Scenario:

While developing the career page, you realize that it is necessary to provide the email addresses of the contacts. Upon request, your co-worker has sent you an Excel worksheet with a list of email addresses.

---

1. Import the Excel worksheet into the web page.

    a. In the document window, scroll down, click at the end of the text "Our Email IDs" and then press **Enter.**

    b. Choose **File→Import→Excel Document.**

    c. If necessary, in the **Import Excel Document** dialog box, navigate to the C:\ 084502Data\Designing Web Pages\Our Global Company folder.

    d. Select **Email IDs.xls** and click **Open.**

    e. In the **Dreamweaver** message box, click **OK.**

    f. Observe that the data in the worksheet has been imported into the web page.

---

2. Preview the web page in a browser.

    a. Choose **File→Save.**

    b. Choose **File→Preview in Browser→IExplore** to preview the web page in Internet Explorer.

    c. Scroll down to view the imported content.

    d. Close the Internet Explorer window.

    e. Close the career.html file.

TOPIC G
Organize Files and Folders

You imported data from other applications into your web pages. You may now want to organize the files in different folders so that they can be easily identified and accessed. In this topic, you will organize files and folders using the **FILES** panel.

While working on multiple files in a single folder, locating a particular file could be difficult. By organizing these files into different folders according to the work flow, you will be able to access them easily. Also, grouping files based on their development status will help you distinguish the files that you are currently working with from the rest.

How to Organize Files and Folders

Procedure Reference: Create a Folder in a Defined Site

To create a folder in a defined site:

1. If necessary, from the **FILES** panel options menu, choose **Expand Files Panel.**
2. From the drop-down list below the **FILES** panel toolbar, select the desired site.
3. If necessary, expand the selected folder.
4. If necessary, collapse the selected folder.
5. Select the folder in which you want to create a folder.
6. Create a folder in the defined site.
    - In the **FILES** panel, right-click the folder and choose **New Folder** or;
    - From the **FILES** panel options menu, choose **File→New Folder.**
7. Type a name for the new folder and press **Enter.**

Procedure Reference: Create a File

To create a file:

1. In the **FILES** panel, select the folder in which you want to create a file.
2. Create a file.
    - In the **FILES** panel, right-click the folder and choose **New File** or;
    - From the **FILES** panel options menu, choose **File→New File.**
3. Type a name for the new file and press **Enter.**

Procedure Reference: Move Files into a Folder

To move files into a folder:

1. In the **FILES** panel, select the file that you want to move into a folder.
2. If necessary, hold down **Ctrl** and select the other files.
3. Drag the selected files into the desired folder.
4. In the **Update Files** dialog box, click **Update** to update the links in the moved files.

ACTIVITY 3-10
Organizing Files and Folders

Data Files:

contactinfo.html, contactus.html, trademarks.html, news_image.jpg, contact_image.jpg

Scenario:

As you build your website, you notice that the number of files used on the website has increased. Most of the files are placed in the root folder and you find it difficult to locate the files.

1.   Move the images from the root folder to the images folder.

    a.   In the **FILES** panel, click the **Expand to show local and remote sites** button.

    b.   Expand the images folder to view the files within it.

    c.   Within the root folder, select **contact_image.jpg,** hold down **Ctrl,** and select **news_image.jpg.**

    d.   Drag the selected files from the news_image.jpg file to the images folder.

Local Files	Size	Type
⊟ 🗁 Site - Our Global Com…		Folder
⊟ images		Folder
🖼 banner_head…	82KB	JPEG Im…

    e.   In the **Update Files** dialog box, click **Update** to update the links in the files.

    f.   Collapse the images folder.

2.   Create a folder.

    a.   Select the **Site - Our Global Company** root folder.

    b.   Choose **File→New Folder** to create a folder.

    c.   Type *Info* and press **Enter.**

3.   Move the contactinfo.html, contactus.html, and trademarks.html files into the Info folder.

    a.   Select **contactinfo.html,** hold down **Ctrl,** and select the **contactus.html** and **trademarks.html** files.

    b.   Drag the selected files from the trademarks.html file to the **Info** folder and in the **Update Files** dialog box, click **Update** to update the links in the files.

    c.   In the **FILES** panel, click the **Collapse to show only local or remote site** button.

Lesson 3 Follow-up

In this lesson, you designed web pages and modified them with graphics and tables. You also formatted a page with CSS and imported data from other applications. Having these skills will help you present effective and visually pleasing information on the web.

1. **Which image format options do you think you might use for your web pages? Why?**

2. **What are the various CSS rules that you might use to enhance the appearance of your web pages? Why?**

4 | Creating Reusable Site Assets

Lesson Time: 1 hour(s), 20 minutes

Lesson Objectives:

In this lesson, you will create reusable site assets.

You will:

- Create and use library items.
- Update library items.
- Use snippets.
- Create a template.

Introduction

You created web pages with various page elements. Now, you are ready to work with page elements to reuse them across different pages. In this lesson, you will create reusable site assets.

While creating web pages, you may find that you have to reuse certain elements across different pages. Creating and modifying them repeatedly is time consuming, and can also be monotonous. You can simplify your work and save time by storing these elements and reusing them whenever required.

This lesson covers all or part of the following Adobe Web Communication using Dreamweaver CS5 objectives:

- Topic A
  - Objective 3.4a: Demonstrate knowledge of the Site and Favorites lists on the Assets panel
  - Objective 3.4b: Identify types of content that can be accessed by using the Assets panel
  - Objective 3.4c: Demonstrate knowledge of how to apply assets from the Assets panel to a web page
- Topic D
  - Objective 2.1b: Identify techniques used to maintain consistency
  - Objective 5.5a: Demonstrate knowledge of Dreamweaver templates

■ Objective 5.5b: Demonstrate knowledge of how to create a new Dreamweaver template

■ Objective 5.5c: Demonstrate knowledge of how to save an existing HTML file as a Dreamweaver template

■ Objective 5.5d: Demonstrate knowledge of how to create and edit editable regions on a template

■ Objective 5.5e: Demonstrate knowledge of how to apply or build pages from templates, and how to detach a template from a page

TOPIC A
Create and Use Library Items

You added different elements to web pages. Now, you may want to use some of the elements on a web page on other pages of the website. In this topic, you will utilize library items.

During the development of a website, there will be situations where you may have to present the same content in several places, such as banner images, links, and so on. Adding this content manually on each place and updating any changes to the content can use up a lot of unnecessary time. You could lessen your workload if you store commonly used content in the library and reuse the content wherever required.

The ASSETS Panel

The **ASSETS** panel is used to view and manage assets on a website. Assets are organized into categories such as images, colors, URLs, media objects, scripts, templates, and libraries. Assets in each category can be viewed using the **Site** option, which displays all the assets, or the **Favorites** option, which displays only the items that have been added as favorites. The **ASSETS** panel provides options to insert and edit assets and manage favorites. It also provides options to add, edit, delete, and apply templates and library items.

Libraries

A *library* is a collection of assets that can be placed on web pages. Each website has its own library. Assets stored in the library are called library items, which can include elements such as tables, images, text, and Flash files. However, style sheets cannot be saved in a library. When a library item is updated, Dreamweaver automatically updates the changes on all the web pages where the library item was used.

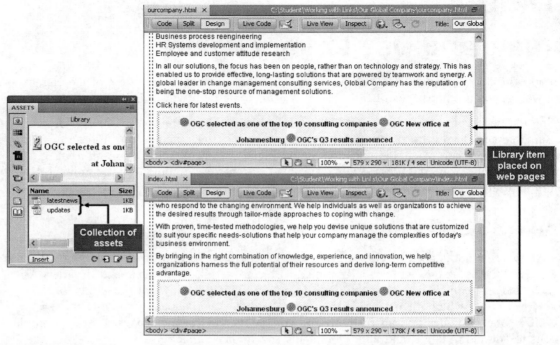

Figure 4-1: *An example of a library item from the ASSETS panel being used in two different document pages.*

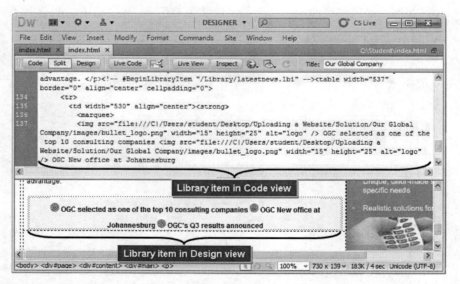

Figure 4-2: *The display of a library item in Design and Code view.*

Library Files

Library items are saved as separate files, with the extension .lbi, in a subfolder named **Library** in the root folder of the defined site. This subfolder is automatically created by Dreamweaver. When a site is uploaded, the **Library** subfolder and the library files in it are not required to be uploaded.

Tags in Library Items

When you create a library item, it must contain a complete set of tags that define the element; all opening tags along with their closing tags must be included. For example, if a table is to be stored as a library item, a complete set of tags defining the table must be included. It is not possible to store just a portion of an element or an object as a library item.

How to Create and Use Library Items

Procedure Reference: Create a Library Item

To create a library item:

1. Display the **ASSETS** panel.
   - Choose **Window→Assets** or;
   - In the **ASSETS** panel group, select the **ASSETS** panel.
2. In the **ASSETS** panel, click the **Library** button.
3. If necessary, in the document window, select the item that needs to be included as a library item.
4. Create a file for the library item.
   - From the **ASSETS** panel options menu, choose **New Library Item.**
   - In the **ASSETS** panel, click the **New Library Item** button.
   - Drag the selected item to the library category list box in the **ASSETS** panel.
   - Choose **Modify→Library→Add Object to Library** or;
   - Right-click in the library category list box in the **ASSETS** panel and choose **New Library Item.**
5. If necessary, in the **Dreamweaver** message box, click **OK.**
6. Type a name for the library item and press **Enter.**
7. If necessary, add content to the library item.
   a. In the **ASSETS** panel, select the library item.
   b. Open the library item in the document window.
      - From the **ASSETS** panel options menu, choose **Edit.**
      - In the **ASSETS** panel, click the **Edit** button or;
      - In the **ASSETS** panel, in the library category list box, right-click the selected library item and choose **Edit.**
   c. In the document window, add the desired content and page elements.
8. Choose **File→Save** to save the library item.

 When a text object is declared as a library item, it is highlighted in Design view with yellow background. Whether or not a background is available for a library item, it still appears with yellow background. If it is an image or an element with a background color, the highlighted part will not appear in Design view. However, in Code view the code section for the library item will always be highlighted. You can change the highlight color by using the **Library items** option in the **Highlighting** category of the **Preferences** dialog box.

Procedure Reference: Rename a Library Item

To rename a library item:

1. If necessary, in the **ASSETS** panel, click the **Library** button.
2. Select the desired library item.
3. Select the name of the item.
   - From the **ASSETS** panel options menu, choose **Rename** or;
   - Right-click the selected library item and choose **Rename.**
4. Type a name and press **Enter.**

Procedure Reference: Delete a Library Item

To delete a library item:

1. In the library category list box of the **ASSETS** panel, select the library item.
2. Delete the library item.
   - Press **Delete.**
   - In the **ASSETS** panel, click the **Delete** button.
   - From the **ASSETS** panel options menu, choose **Delete** or;
   - Right-click the selected item and choose **Delete.**
3. In the **Dreamweaver** message box, click **Yes.**

 When a library item is deleted, it is removed from the library, but not from the pages where it has been placed.

 A deleted library item can be recreated in the library by selecting its instance on any page where it has been used and by using the **Recreate** option in the **PROPERTIES** panel.

Procedure Reference: Place a Library Item on Site Pages

To place a library item on site pages:

1. In the document window, click at the point where the library item needs to be placed.
2. Display the **ASSETS** panel.
3. In the **ASSETS** panel, select the library item that needs to be placed on the web page.
4. Place the library item on the web page.
   - In the **ASSETS** panel, click **Insert.**
   - From the **ASSETS** panel options menu, choose **Insert.**
   - Drag the library item to the desired location on the web page or;
   - Right-click the library item and choose **Insert.**
5. If necessary, select the inserted library item, and in the **PROPERTIES** panel, click **Detach from original** to edit this instance of the library item, or prevent this instance of the library item from being updated when the library item is modified.

ACTIVITY 4-1
Creating Library Items from Site Pages

Data Files:

index.html

Before You Begin:

If the Our Global Company site was previously defined in Dreamweaver, you must modify the Local Root folder and the Default images folder in the site definition so that it is based on the new data from the C:\084502Data\Creating Reusable Site Assets\Our Global Company folder.

Scenario:

The marketing head of your company is impressed with the website you created. He suggested that the news headlines flashed across the home page be shown on other pages too so that visitors will not miss the latest news from your company.

---

1. Select the content for the library item.

   a. In the **FILES** panel, expand **Site - Our Global Company.**

   b. Double-click **index.html** to open the file.

   c. In the document window, scroll down to the end of the page.

   d. At the bottom of the page, in the container above the footer information, click before the text "OGC," hold down **Shift,** and click after the text "Johannesburg" to select the text.

---

2. Create a library item from the selection.

   a. In the **FILES** panel group, select the **ASSETS** panel.

   b. In the **ASSETS** panel, click the **Library** button. 🔲

   c. At the bottom of the **ASSETS** panel, click the **New Library Item** button. 🔲

   d. If necessary, in the **Dreamweaver** message box, click **OK.**

   e. In the **ASSETS** panel, observe that a library item is created and the default name is selected.

   f. Type *latestnews* and press **Enter.**

   g. Choose **File→Save All** to save the library item and the web page.

   h. On the index.html document tab, click the close button to close the file.

ACTIVITY 4-2
Placing Library Items on Site Pages

Data Files:

ourcompany.html

Before You Begin:

In the **FILES** panel, double-click **ourcompany.html** to open it.

Scenario:

Having created a library item for the news headlines on the home page, you decide to include the item uniformly on all the site pages. You need to ensure that the news headlines are displayed consistently across all the pages of the website.

---

1. Place the news headlines on the web page.

   a. In the document window, scroll down to the bottom of the page.

   b. Above the footer information, click in the announcement container.

   c. In the **ASSETS** panel, select **latestnews** and click **Insert.**

   d. Observe that the news headlines are inserted on the web page.

---

2. Preview the web page in a browser.

   a. In the document window, click below the news headlines library item to deselect it.

   b. Save the file.

   c. On the **Document** toolbar, click the **Preview/Debug in browser** button and choose **Preview in IExplore** to preview the web page in Internet Explorer.

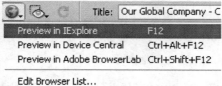

   d. Scroll down to the bottom of the page.

   e. Observe the news headlines on the page.

   f. Close the Internet Explorer window.

   g. On the ourcompany.html document tab, click the close button to close the file.

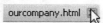

TOPIC B
Update Library Items

You created library items and placed them on web pages. You may sometimes find the need to modify them and update the changes on all the web pages. In this topic, you will update library items.

You may have created a library item from an element that appears in multiple pages of your website, and you may find it necessary to make changes to the element. By modifying the library item and updating it, you will be able to make the change across the website, thereby ensuring uniformity on your website.

How to Update Library Items

Procedure Reference: Modify a Library Item

To modify a library item:

1. In the **ASSETS** panel, in the library category list box, select the library item that needs to be modified.
2. Open the library item.
   - In the **ASSETS** panel, click the **Edit** button.
   - From the **ASSETS** panel options menu, choose **Edit**.
   - Right-click the library item and choose **Edit** or;
   - Double-click the library item.
3. In the document window, make the necessary changes to the library item.
4. Choose **File→Save**.
5. If necessary, update the library items.
   a. In the **Update library Items** dialog box, click **Update**.

 This dialog box is displayed only when the library item is used on other pages of the website.

   b. In the **Update Pages** dialog box, from the **Look in** drop-down list, select the desired option.
      - Select **Files That Use** to update the web pages that use the library item.
      - Select **Entire Site** and from the drop-down list displayed on the right, select the site name to update the pages using the library item on the site.
   c. If necessary, uncheck the **Library items** check box to avoid updating the library items.
   d. If necessary, uncheck the **Templates** check box to avoid updating the templates.
   e. If necessary, check the **Show log** check box to view information about the updating of the web pages.
   f. Click **Start** to start updating the pages.
   g. Click **Close** to close the **Update Pages** dialog box.

6. If necessary, click **Don't Update** to avoid updating the web pages using the library item.

Procedure Reference: Update a Specific Web Page with Changes to Library Items

To update a specific web page with changes to library items:

1. Open the web page in which the library item is to be updated.
2. Update the library item on the page.
   - Choose **Modify→Library→Update Current Page.**
   - In the **ASSETS** panel, in the library category list box, right-click the library item and choose **Update Current Page** or;
   - From the **ASSETS** panel options menu, choose **Update Current Page.**

Procedure Reference: Update an Entire Website with Changes to Library Items

To update an entire website with the changes to library items:

1. Display the **Update Pages** dialog box.
   - Choose **Modify→Library→Update Pages.**
   - In the **ASSETS** panel, right-click in the library category list box and choose **Update Site** or;
   - From the **ASSETS** panel options menu, choose **Update Site.**
2. If necessary, from the drop-down list to the right of the **Look in** drop-down list, select the site name or the library item.

 Depending on the option you select from the **Look in** drop-down list, options in the adjacent drop-down list also change.

3. If necessary, set the desired options.
4. Click **Start** to start updating the pages.
5. If necessary, click **Stop** to stop the updating process.
6. Click **Close** to close the **Update Pages** dialog box.

ACTIVITY 4-3
Updating Library Items

Data Files:

index.html, ourcompany.html

Scenario:

You placed the library item for news headlines on your web pages. Your company has recently announced its third quarter results and you need to include this information on the web pages.

---

1. Modify the news headlines library item.

    a. In the **ASSETS** panel, in the library category list box, select **latestnews**.

    b. At the bottom of the **ASSETS** panel, click the **Edit** button.

    c. Click after the text "OGC," hold down **Shift,** click at the end of the text, and press **Delete.**

    d. Type **'s Q3 results announced**

    e. Choose **File→Save.**

---

2. Update the library item on all pages.

    a. In the **Update Library Items** dialog box, click **Update.**

    b. In the **Update Pages** dialog box, from the **Look in** drop-down list, select **Entire Site.**

    c. In the drop-down list to the right of the **Look in** drop-down list, verify that **Our Global Company** is selected.

    d. In the **Update** section, verify that the **Library items** check box is checked and then click **Start** to start updating the pages.

    e. Click **Close.**

---

3. Preview the updated pages in a browser.

    a. In the **FILES** panel, double-click **index.html.**

    b. On the **Document** toolbar, click the **Preview/Debug in browser** button and choose **Preview in IExplore** to preview the web page in Internet Explorer.

    c. Observe that the news headlines are updated.

    d. Close the Internet Explorer window.

    e. Choose **File→Close All** to close all open files.

TOPIC C

Use Snippets

You updated library items on multiple pages of your website. Sometimes, you may need to use specific content or a piece of code in more than one page. In this topic, you will use snippets to store and reuse page elements.

While working on a website, you use not only text and images frequently but also the same code in different pages. Rewriting code repeatedly is a time-consuming task; saving the code makes it comfortable for you to reuse it wherever required. Using snippets, you can store and reuse code.

Snippets

Definition:

Snippets are stored blocks of code that can be used on web pages. They help you save time by avoiding the task of having to retype code. You can create, edit, and insert snippets wherever they are required. Editing a snippet does not update any previous insertions of that snippet, because Dreamweaver does not maintain a link between a snippet inserted on a page and the original snippet. You can create snippets using coding languages such as CSS, XHTML, or JavaScript. You can also use a set of predefined snippets organized into folders by functionality.

Example:

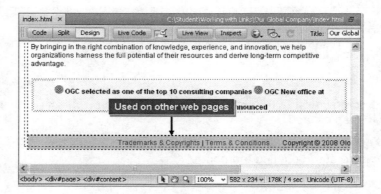

Differentiation Between Library Items and Snippets

Library items and snippets have similar functionality; you can use both these components repeatedly across pages in documents without having to create them from scratch every time. But there is a major difference between the two. When a library item is updated, Dreamweaver automatically updates the changes on all the web pages where the library item had been used. Editing a snippet does not update any previous insertions of that snippet, because Dreamweaver does not maintain a link between a snippet inserted on a page and the original snippet.

The SNIPPETS Panel

The *SNIPPETS panel* allows you to view and manage snippets on a website. It provides options for creating snippet folders, as well as inserting, creating, editing, and deleting snippets. This panel displays a list of predefined and user-defined snippets that can be inserted on web pages. The predefined snippets are organized into folders based on various categories. You can create snippets that can be wrapped around a selection or inserted as a block, and preview a snippet either as code or design.

How to Use Snippets

Procedure Reference: Create Snippets

To create snippets:

1. Display the **SNIPPETS** panel.
    - Choose **Window→Snippets.**
    - In the **SNIPPETS** panel group, select the **SNIPPETS** panel or;
    - In the **SNIPPETS** panel group, double-click the **SNIPPETS** panel.
2. If necessary, create a folder.
    a. Create a folder.
        - From the **SNIPPETS** panel options menu, choose **New Folder.**
        - In the **SNIPPETS** panel, click the **New Snippet Folder** button or;
        - In the bottom pane of the **SNIPPETS** panel, right-click and choose **New Folder.**
    b. Type a name for the folder and press **Enter.**
3. If necessary, select the folder in which the new snippet is to be stored.
4. If necessary, select the desired content or code to be saved as a new snippet.
    - In Code view, select the block of code.
    - In Design view, select the section of the web page for which you want to save the code.
5. Display the **Snippet** dialog box.
    - From the **SNIPPETS** panel options menu, choose **New Snippet** or;
    - In the **SNIPPETS** panel, click the **New Snippet** button.
6. In the **Name** text box, type a name for the snippet.
7. In the **Description** text box, type a description of the snippet.
8. Specify the snippet type.
    - Create a wrap selection snippet type.
        a. In the **Snippet type** section, select **Wrap selection** to specify two blocks of code to surround the selected code when inserted.
        b. If necessary, in the **Insert before** text box, type the code that will appear before the selected code.
        c. If necessary, in the **Insert after** text box, type the code that will appear after the selected code.
    - Create an insert block snippet type.

      a.   In the **Snippet type** section, select **Insert block** to specify a single block of code that will appear in a specific location when inserted.

      b.   If necessary, in the **Insert code** text box, type the desired code.

9.   In the **Preview type** section, specify the preview type of the snippet.

- Select **Design** to display the snippet design in the top pane of the **SNIPPETS** panel.
- Select **Code** to display the snippet code in the top pane of the **SNIPPETS** panel.

10. Click **OK** to create the snippet.

Procedure Reference: Insert a Snippet

To insert a snippet:

1.   Open the web page on which the snippet needs to be inserted.
2.   In the document window, click at the location where the snippet needs to be inserted.
3.   If necessary, in the **SNIPPETS** panel, expand the folder in which the snippet is saved.
4.   Select the snippet.
5.   Insert the snippet in the document.

- In the **SNIPPETS** panel, click **Insert.**
- Double-click the snippet.
- Right-click the snippet and choose **Insert** or;
- Drag the snippet to the desired location.

Procedure Reference: Edit a Snippet

To edit a snippet:

1.   In the **SNIPPETS** panel, select the snippet that needs to be edited.
2.   Display the **Snippets** dialog box.

- Right-click the snippet and choose **Edit.**
- From the **SNIPPETS** panel options menu, choose **Edit** or;
- In the **SNIPPETS** panel, click the **Edit Snippet** button.

3.   Make the necessary changes.
4.   Click **OK** to save the changes.

Procedure Reference: Delete a Snippet

To delete a snippet:

1.   In the **SNIPPETS** panel, select the desired snippet.
2.   Delete the snippet.

- From the **SNIPPETS** panel options menu, choose **Delete.**
- In the **SNIPPETS** panel, click the **Remove** button or,
- Right-click the snippet and choose **Delete.**

ACTIVITY 4-4
Using Snippets

Data Files:

index.html, ourcompany.html

Before You Begin:

In the **FILES** panel, double-click **index.html** to open it.

Scenario:

You have footer information on the home page. You also know that this information will be reused across all other pages of your website.

---

1. Save the footer as a snippet.

    a. Choose **Window→Snippets.**

    b. In the **SNIPPETS** panel, right-click below the Legacy folder and choose **New Folder.**

    c. Type *OGC* and press **Enter.**

    d. In the document window, scroll down to the bottom of the page, click before the word "Trademarks," hold down **Shift,** and click at the end of the word "Inc."

    e. In the **SNIPPETS** panel, click the **New Snippet** button, [icon] to display the **Snippet** dialog box.

    f. In the **Name** text box, type *OGC_Footer*

    g. In the **Description** text box, click and type *Our Global Company Footer*

    h. Click **OK** to create the snippet.

    i. In the **SNIPPETS** panel, verify that the **OGC_Footer** snippet is stored in the **OGC** snippet folder.

    j. Close the index.html file.

---

2. Insert the snippet on the **ourcompany.html** page.

    a. In the **FILES** panel, double-click **ourcompany.html** to open it.

    b. In the document window, scroll down to the bottom of the page and click in the container for the footer.

    c. In the **SNIPPETS** panel, select **OGC_Footer** and click **Insert.**

    d. Verify that the snippet is inserted into the container for the footer of the web page.

    e. Save the file.

    f. Close the ourcompany.html file.

TOPIC D

Create a Template

You created snippets and reused them on other pages where they were needed. You may also want to reuse certain larger sections of your page and ensure consistency in the appearance of the web pages. In this topic, you will create templates.

Sometimes, you may want certain information to appear consistently on all pages of a website. Moreover, whenever there is a change in the information, updating the changes on each page can be cumbersome and time consuming. Being able to work with templates minimizes the effort expended on creating and maintaining web pages with similar formats.

Templates

Definition:

A *template* is a document that contains predefined design elements such as graphics and text. It can also contain functional settings such as links. Using a template, you can create web pages that share common design elements. Templates can be modified according to your preferences.

Example:

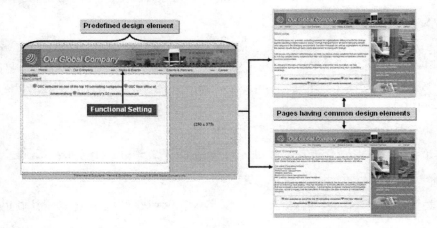

Advantages of Templates

Templates allow you to build master pages, on which other pages can be built, ensuring that common page elements are always in the same position and appear consistently across pages. You can specify only certain areas of the template as editable, thereby protecting other areas from accidental changes or deletions. Also, updating a template will cause all other pages to be updated, saving you valuable time and effort and ensuring consistency across the pages of a site.

Regions of a Template

In Dreamweaver templates, you can define regions that aid in the development of web pages. The following table describes those regions.

Region	Description
Non-editable	Remains locked and therefore the elements in it cannot be modified. By default, the entire area in a template is non-editable.
Editable	Contains elements that can be modified according to the user's preferences.
Repeating	Can be replicated any number of times based on the user's preferences.
Optional	Can be shown or hidden according to the user's preferences.

How to Create a Template

Procedure Reference: Create a Template from a Web Page

To create a template from a web page:
1. Open the desired web page.
2. If necessary, add the desired elements required for the template.
3. Choose **File→Save As Template.**
4. In the **Save As Template** dialog box, from the **Site** drop-down list, select the desired site in which the template is to be saved.
5. If necessary, in the **Description** text box, type a description of the template.
6. In the **Save As** text box, type a name for the template.
7. Click **Save** to save the template.

 Dreamweaver templates are saved with the file extension .dwt. All templates created for a defined site are saved in a subfolder, named **Templates**, which is created in the root folder.

8. In the **Dreamweaver** message box, click **Yes.**

Procedure Reference: Create a Template from a Blank Template

To create a template from a blank template:
1. Choose **File→New.**
2. In the **New Document** dialog box, select the **Blank Template** category.
3. In the **Template Type** list box, select **HTML template.**
4. If necessary, in the **Layout** list box, select the desired layout.
5. Click **Create.**
6. Add the content that is to be replicated across pages on the new template.
7. Choose **File→Save.**

8.   In the **Dreamweaver** message box, click **OK.**

Procedure Reference: Define a Region in a Template

To define a region in a template:

1.   In the template, place the insertion point in the desired location.

2.   Define the selected region.

- ●   Define an editable region.

     a.   Choose **Insert→Template Objects→Editable Region.**

     b.   In the **New Editable Region** dialog box, in the **Name** text box, type a name for the region.

     c.   Click **OK.**

- ●   Define an optional region.

     a.   Choose **Insert→Template Objects→Optional Region.**

     b.   In the **New Optional Region** dialog box, in the **Name** text box, type a name for the region.

     c.   If necessary, uncheck the **Show by Default** check box.

     d.   Click **OK.**

- ●   Define a repeating region.

     a.   Choose **Insert→Template Objects→Repeating Region.**

     b.   In the **New Repeating Region** dialog box, in the **Name** text box, type a name for the region.

     c.   Click **OK.**

     d.   Within the repeating region, place the insertion point at the desired location where an editable region needs to be defined.

     e.   Define the editable regions within the repeating region.

3.   Save and close the template.

Procedure Reference: Create a Page from a Template

To create a page from a template:

1.   Choose **File→New.**

2.   In the **New Document** dialog box, select the **Page from Template** category.

3.   In the **Site** list box, select the site that contains the template based on which you want to create a web page.

4.   In the **Template for Site "<Site Name>"** list box, select the desired template.

5.   If necessary, uncheck the **Update page when template changes** check box.

6.   Click **Create** to create a page based on the template.

7. If necessary, add the repeating region data.

    a. In the repeating region header, click the plus button (+) to add a row.

    b. Add content to the editable region within the repeating region.

    c. If necessary, add more rows and content.

    d. If necessary, click in a cell of the desired row and in the repeating region header, click the Minus button (-) to delete the row.

    e. If necessary, click in a cell of the desired row and in the repeating region header, click the Up Arrow button or the Down Arrow button to move the row up or down.

Procedure Reference: Apply a Template to a Web Page

To apply a template to a web page:

1. Open the web page to which you want to apply a template.

2. In the **ASSETS** panel, on the left side, click the **Templates** button.

3. In the templates category list box, select the desired template.

4. Apply the template.

    ● Select the template.

        a. Choose **Modify→Templates→Apply Template to Page.**

        b. If necessary, in the **Select Template** dialog box, from the **Site** drop-down list, select the site in which the desired template is defined.

        c. In the **Templates** list box, select the desired template.

        d. Click **Select.**

    ● In the **ASSETS** panel, click **Apply** to apply the selected template to the page.

    ● In the templates category list box, right-click and choose **Apply** or;

    ● From the **ASSETS** panel options menu, choose **Apply.**

5. If necessary, specify the region on the template to which you want to move the required content of the web page.

    a. In the **Inconsistent Region Names** dialog box, in the list box, select the desired region of the web page.

    b. From the **Move content to new region** drop-down list, select the region of the template in which you want the selected content to appear.

    c. Click **OK.**

Procedure Reference: Modify a Template

To modify a template:

1. Open the desired template.

2. Make the desired changes to the template.

3. Choose **File→Save.**

4. In the **Update Template Files** dialog box, click **Update** to reflect the changes on all the web pages that were created based on this template.

5. In the **Update Pages** dialog box, click **Close.**

The Detach from Template Option

The **Detach from Template** option allows you to detach a web page from the original template. When you detach a web page, the regions defined in the original template are no longer applicable. When you modify a template and update pages based on the template, pages that are detached from the template will not be updated.

ACTIVITY 4-5
Creating a Template

Data Files:

layout.html, Terms.txt

Before You Begin:

1. Navigate to the C:\084502Data\Creating Reusable Site Assets\Our Global company folder and open the Terms.txt file in Notepad.

2. Switch to the Dreamweaver application.

3. In the **FILES** panel, double-click **layout.html** to open it.

Scenario:

You want to create web pages for your site similar to the one you created. A number of elements on the web page must appear consistently on all pages of the website, while the content in other sections of the web pages will vary and be editable.

---

1. Create a template using the layout.html file.

   a. Observe that the page contains the company logo, header banner image, and a menu below the header image.

   b. Choose **File→Save as Template.**

   c. In the **Save As Template** dialog box, in the **Save as** text box, type *OGC_layout*

   d. In the **Description** text box, click and type *Our Global Company template*

   e. Click **Save** to save the web page as a template.

   f. In the **Dreamweaver** message box, click **Yes.**

---

2. Define the editable region in the template.

   a. Click in the empty container below the header.

   b. Choose **Insert→Template Objects→Editable Region.**

   c. In the **New Editable Region** dialog box, in the **Name** text box, type *MainContent* to name the editable region.

   d. Click **OK.**

   e. In the document window, observe that an editable region is defined.

   f. Save the OGC_layout.dwt template file.

   g. Close the file.

---

3. Create a web page based on the template.

   a. Choose **File→New.**

---

    b.   In the **New Document** dialog box, select the **Page from Template** category.

    c.   In the **Site** list box, verify that **Our Global Company** is selected and in the **Template for Site "Our Global Company"** list box, verify that **OGC_layout** is selected.

    d.   Verify that the **Update page when template changes** check box is checked and click **Create.**

4.   Add content to the web page.

    a.   Switch to the Terms.txt file.

    b.   In the Notepad window, choose **Edit→Select All.**

    c.   Choose **Edit→Copy.**

    d.   Switch to the Dreamweaver application.

    e.   In the document window, in the **MainContent** editable region, double-click the text **"MainContent"** to select it.

    f.   Choose **Edit→Paste.**

    g.   Choose **File→Save.**

    h.   If necessary, in the **Save As** dialog box, navigate to the C:\084502Data\Creating Reusable Site Assets\Our Global Company\Info folder.

    i.   In the **File name** text box, click and type *Terms* and then click **Save.**

    j.   Close the file.

    k.   Close the Terms.txt file.

ACTIVITY 4-6
Creating a Repeating Region Template

Data Files:

eventupdates.html

Before You Begin:

In the **FILES** panel, double-click **eventupdates.html** to open it.

Scenario:

You need to create a web page displaying the upcoming events in which your company will be involved. As you may have to update the events on this page quite often, you want the table adjustable enough to be expanded whenever it is required.

---

1. Create a region in the template that can be expanded with multiple insertions.

    a. Click in the first cell of the second row of the table.

    b. Hold down **Shift** and click in the third cell of the second row.

    c. Choose **Insert→Template Objects→Repeating Region.**

    d. In the **Dreamweaver** message box, check the **Don't show me this message again** check box and click **OK.**

    e. In the **New Repeating Region** dialog box, in the **Name** text box, type *Events* and click **OK.**

---

2. Add editable regions within the repeating region.

    a. Click in the first cell of the second row and choose **Insert→Template Objects→ Editable Region.**

    b. In the **New Editable Region** dialog box, in the **Name** text box, type *Date* and click **OK.**

    c. Add an editable region in the second cell named *Event* and another editable region in the third cell of the last row named *Venue*

    d. Choose **File→Save as Template.**

    e. In the **Save As Template** dialog box, in the **Save as** text box, verify that **eventupdates** is displayed and click **Save.**

    f. In the **Dreamweaver** message box, click **Yes.**

    g. Close the template file.

---

3. Create a document based on the repeating region template.

    a. Choose **File→New.**

    b. In the **New Document** dialog box, verify that the **Page from Template** category is selected, and in the **Site** list box, verify that **Our Global Company** is selected.

---

    c.   In the **Template for Site "Our Global Company"** list box, verify that **eventupdates** is selected and click **Create.**

4. Create repeating rows and enter content.

    a.   In the second row, in the **Date** editable region, double-click and type *Aug 15* and then press **Tab.**

    b.   In the **Event** editable region, type *Six Sigma Workshop* and press **Tab.**

    c.   In the **Venue** editable region, type *The Knowledge Center, New York*

    d.   In the **Repeat: Events** header of the repeating region, click the plus button (+) to add a row.

    e.   In the new row, add the following details.
- Date: *Sep 02*
- Event: *National Convention of Project Consultants*
- Venue: *International Conference Center, Chicago*

    f.   In the **Repeat: Events** header of the repeating region, click the plus button (+) to insert a row.

    g.   In the new row, add the following details.
- Date: *Sep 10*
- Event: *Seminar on Internet and Security*
- Venue: *Boston Convention Hall, Boston*

5. Preview the web page in a browser.

    a.   In the C:\084502Data\Creating Reusable Site Assets\Our Global Company folder, save the file as *upcomingevents.html*

    b.   On the **Document** toolbar, click the **Preview/Debug in browser** button, and choose **Preview in IExplore** to preview the web page in Internet Explorer.

    c.   Close the Internet Explorer window.

    d.   Close the file.

Lesson 4 Follow-up

In this lesson, you worked with reusable site assets such as snippets, library items, and templates. Reusing items simplifies your work and saves time.

1. **For which element on your web page do you think you might create a library item? Why?**

2. **What regions will you define on your template? Why?**

5 | Working with Links

Lesson Time: 1 hour(s), 20 minutes

Lesson Objectives:

In this lesson, you will work with different types of links.

You will:

- Create internal and external hyperlinks.
- Create anchors.
- Create email links.
- Create image maps.
- Create image link rollovers.

Introduction

You created a number of web pages for your site. Now, you are ready to provide navigation between and within those pages. In this lesson, you will create links.

Assume that you are browsing through several pages of a website and want to return to its home page. Without some necessary navigation controls, it would be difficult to move from one page to another. You can make your site user friendly and easy to navigate by providing logical and dependable links at the appropriate locations.

This lesson covers all or part of the following Adobe Web Communication using Dreamweaver CS5 objectives:

- Topic A
    - Objective 4.5a: Demonstrate knowledge of terms "hyperlink," "e-mail link," and "named anchor"
    - Objective 4.5b: Demonstrate knowledge of hyperlinks, including the differences between absolute, site-root-relative, and document-relative hyperlinks
    - Objective 4.5c: Demonstrate knowledge of how to link text and images to another web page of the same site
    - Objective 4.5d: Demonstrate knowledge of how to link text and images to another website
    - Objective 4.5g: Demonstrate knowledge of how to target links
    - Objective 6.5c: Demonstrate knowledge of how to link files by dragging, using the Point-to-File icon in the Properties panel and the Files panel
- Topic B

- ■ Objective 4.5f: Demonstrate knowledge of how to create and link to a named anchor
- ● Topic C
  - ■ Objective 4.5e: Demonstrate knowledge of how to link text or images to an email address
- ● Topic D
  - ■ Objective 4.8a: Demonstrate knowledge of the terms "hotspot" and "image map" as used in web page design
  - ■ Objective 4.8b: Demonstrate knowledge of how to create an image map
  - ■ Objective 4.8c: Identify best practices when creating image maps
  - ■ Objective 4.8d: Demonstrate knowledge of how to set properties for a hotspot by using the Properties panel
- ● Topic E
  - ■ Objective 4.7a: Demonstrate knowledge of how to insert navigation bars, rollover images, and buttons created in Fireworks

TOPIC A
Create Hyperlinks

You used templates to maintain consistency across all pages of a website. Now, you will determine how to provide a navigation system that enables cross referencing of web page content. In this topic, you will create hyperlinks.

Browsing through a website to locate related information could become tedious and frustrating when there are numerous web pages. Providing hyperlinks to different web pages on the site will help visitors easily navigate to the desired page.

Hyperlinks

Definition:

Hyperlinks are links that reference another web page or a file on the same website or a different website. By default, the text that contains a hyperlink is in blue and underlined. When you click a hyperlink, the target web page opens in the same window; it can also be opened in a new window. Hyperlinks can be created for text or images. You can also create hyperlinks to link to files such as PDF documents.

Example:

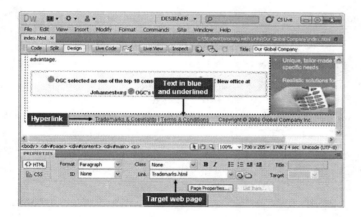

Internal and External Hyperlinks

If the file you are linking is stored in the same folder or directory as the current page, you can use the name of the file as the link. If the file you are linking is stored in a subfolder, you need to provide the path to the file followed by the file name. For example, if you have a file named "newreleases.html" within the "products" folder, the link to that file must be "products/newreleases.html." If the file you are using is in a subfolder, and you are linking another file stored in a different subfolder, you need to provide the path to the file from the root folder followed by the file name. For example, if you are using a file named "octoberevents.html" within the "october" subfolder of the root folder, and you need to link a file named "newevents.html" within the "new" subfolder of the root folder, the link to that file must be "..\new\newevents.html." These links to files within the same site are known as internal hyperlinks or site root-relative hyperlinks.

When the links you create refer to files on another website, you need to specify the domain name along with the file name. For example, if you are linking a file named "contact.html" in the website "www.citizensinfo.org," you will specify the link as "www.citizensinfo.org/contact.html." Links to pages in other websites are known as external hyperlinks or document-relative hyperlinks. Internal and external hyperlinks can be created to other file types, such as PDF, Excel worksheets, and Word documents. For example, if you need to link a PDF file named "Q3report.pdf" stored within the "reports" subfolder, the link to that file must be "reports/Q3report.pdf."

The <a> Tag

The <a> tag is used to create hyperlinks for text and images. To refer to a text or an image on a different web page, you must specify the URL in the `href` attribute. The syntax to create an external hyperlink using the <a> tag is as follows:

```
<a href=URL>Text</a>
```

Pseudo-Class Selectors for the <a> Tag

Dreamweaver provides four pseudo-class selectors for the <a> tag. They are as follows:

- `a:link`—the status of a link that has not been used for navigation.
- `a:visited`—the status of a link after it has been used for navigating.
- `a:hover`—the status of a link when the mouse pointer is positioned over it.
- `a:active`—the status of a link when it is clicked.

While using these pseudo-classes, it is important to list them in the above order to function properly. This is because of the cascading effect of the rules when they are applied.

The Case-Sensitive Link Checking Option

The **Site Definition** wizard contains an option for checking case-sensitive links. This option can be used to ensure that the case of the links matches with that of the file names when Dreamweaver checks the website links. However, this option is useful only on UNIX systems where the file names are case sensitive.

The Hyperlink Dialog Box

The **Hyperlink** dialog box allows you to create links to a web page. It contains several options.

Option	Allows You To
Text	Specify the text with which you want to create a link.
Link	Specify the web page to which you want to create a link. You can also use the **Browse** button to browse and locate the file.

Option	Allows You To
Target	Control how the links should open. • The **_blank** option opens the linked page in a new browser window. • The **_parent** option opens the linked page in a parent frameset. • The **_self** option opens the linked page in the same browser window. • The **_top** option removes all the frames in a window and loads the linked page in the browser window.
Title	Enter a description of the page you are linking. This description appears as a yellow pop-up box in the browser. This is also helpful when people use screen readers.
Access key	Specify a shortcut key to select a link.
Tab index	Specify the tab order.

How to Create Hyperlinks

Procedure Reference: Create Hyperlinks

To create hyperlinks:

1. Select the desired text or image.
2. Create a hyperlink.

   • In the **PROPERTIES** panel, click **HTML** and in the **Link** text box, click and type the file name or the URL to create a hyperlink.

 You must type the full URL for an external hyperlink. To avoid errors, you can copy the link from the browser and paste it in the **Link** text box.

   • In the **PROPERTIES** panel, to the right of the **Link** text box, click and drag the **Point to File** icon to the desired file in the **FILES** panel.
   • Create an internal hyperlink using the **Browse for File** button.

      a. In the **PROPERTIES** panel, to the right of the **Link** text box, click the **Browse for File** button.

      b. In the **Select File** dialog box, navigate to the site folder, select the desired file, and click **OK** or;

   • Create a hyperlink using the **Hyperlink** dialog box.

      a. In the **INSERT** panel, click **Hyperlink**.

      b. In the **Hyperlink** dialog box, create a hyperlink.

         ■ In the **Link** text box, click and type the URL or the file name or;

         ■ To the right of the **Link** text box, click the **Browse** button, navigate to the site folder, select a file, and click **OK**.

3.   If necessary, in the **PROPERTIES** panel, from the **Target** drop-down list, select **_blank** to open the link in a new browser window.

4.   If necessary, verify the hyperlinks in a browser.

    a.   Preview the web page in a browser.

    b.   Click the hyperlink to view the target web page.

    c.   Close the browser window.

ACTIVITY 5-1
Creating Hyperlinks

Data Files:

index.html

Before You Begin:

1. If the Our Global Company site was previously defined in Dreamweaver, you must modify the Local Root folder and Default images folder in the site definition so that it is based on the new data from the C:\084502Data\Working with Links\Our Global Company folder.

2. In the **FILES** panel, expand the **Site - Our Global Company** folder and double-click the **index.html** file.

Scenario:

You have information on the Trademarks and Copyrights and the Terms and Conditions of your company on separate pages. You want visitors to be able to access these pages from the home page. You also need to ensure that any formatting that you apply to the text on this page is consistent with the colors used on the website.

---

1. Create a hyperlink.

    a. Scroll down to the bottom of the page and in the container for the footer, select the text **"Trademarks & Copyrights."**

    b. If necessary, in the **PROPERTIES** panel, click **HTML.**

    c. To the right of the **Link** drop-down list, click the **Browse for File** button.

    d. In the **Select File** dialog box, navigate to the C:\084502Data\Working with Links\Our Global Company\Info folder.

    e. Select **trademarks.html** and click **OK.**

    f. Similarly, link the text "Terms & Conditions" to the terms.html file.

    g. Switch to Code view.

    h. On line **106,** observe the `<a href="Info/terms.html">` tag, which indicates that the terms.html file is located within the **Info** subfolder.

    i. Save the file.

---

2. Verify the hyperlink.

    a. On the **Document** toolbar, click the **Preview/Debug in browser** button and choose **Preview in IExplore.**

    b. If necessary, maximize the Internet Explorer window.

    c. Click the **Trademarks & Copyrights** link to view the trademarks and copyrights information.

d.   In Internet Explorer, click **Back.**

e.   Click the **Terms & Conditions** link to view the terms and conditions information.

f.   Close the Internet Explorer window.

3.   Set and apply CSS properties to the links.

a.   Switch to Design view.

b.   In the **PROPERTIES** panel, click **Page Properties.**

c.   In the **Page Properties** dialog box, in the **Category** list box, select **Links (CSS).**

d.   In the **Links (CSS)** section, in the **Link color** text box, click and type *#333333*

e.   In the **Rollover links** text box, click and type *#4C70A2*

f.   In the **Visited links** text box, click and type *#8E8E8E*

g.   In the **Active links** text box, click and type *#569DC9*

h.   From the **Underline style** drop-down list, select **Show underline only on rollover.**

i.   Click **OK** to apply the CSS properties to the page.

4.   Preview the web page in a browser.

a.   Save the file.

b.   On the **Document** toolbar, click the **Preview/Debug in browser** button and choose **Preview in IExplore.**

c.   Maximize the Internet Explorer window.

d.   Place the mouse pointer over the "Trademarks & Copyrights" link to view the link color on mouseover.

e.   Close the Internet Explorer window.

f.   Close the index.html file.

TOPIC B
Create Anchors

You have created links to different web pages. You can also create links to a particular section within a web page. In this topic, you will create anchors.

Assume that you have an exhaustive amount of information on your web page. When users need to locate particular information on a page, they may have to go through the entire content to locate it. By providing links at appropriate locations, you can enable users to navigate directly to the information they are interested in.

Anchors

An *anchor* is a link that takes visitors to a particular location on a page. You can create a named anchor for each section or heading and provide links to it at suitable locations on the web page. Anchors help users quickly return to a section without having to scroll through the page.

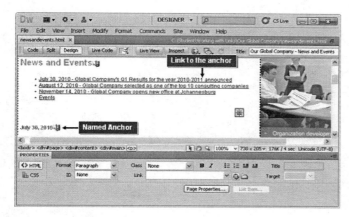

Figure 5-1: Anchors used on a web page.

How to Create Anchors

Procedure Reference: Create Anchor Links

To create anchor links:

1. In the document window, place the insertion point before the text for which you want to create an anchor.

2. Open the **Named Anchor** dialog box.

    *   In the **INSERT** panel, click **Named Anchor** or;

    *   Choose **Insert→Named Anchor.**

3. In the **Anchor name** text box, type a name and click **OK** to create an anchor.

4. Select the text to which you want to link the anchor.

5. Create a link to the named anchor.

    *   In the **PROPERTIES** panel, in the **Link** text box, click and type **#** and then the anchor name to create a link to the named anchor.

    *   In the **PROPERTIES** panel, to the right of the **Link** text box, click the **Point to File** button and drag it to the anchor marker on the web page or;

    *   Create a link using the **Hyperlink** dialog box.

        ▪   In the **Link** text box, click and type **#** and then the anchor name or;

        ▪   From the **Link** drop-down list, select the desired anchor.

 You can also link a named anchor on another page by typing the file name, then the **#** sign, and then the named anchor. For example, the code `<a href="newreleases.html#march">March Releases</a>` will take you to the section "March Releases" in the file newreleases.html.

6. If necessary, verify the anchor links in a browser.
    a.   Preview the web page in a browser.
    b.   Click an anchor link to move to a particular section on the web page.
    c.   Close the browser window.

ACTIVITY 5-2
Creating Anchor Links

Data Files:

newsandevents.html, ourcompany.html

Before You Begin:

In the **FILES** panel, double-click the **newsandevents.html** file to open it.

Scenario:

You have a list of the latest news and events in the newsandevents.html file. You do not want your visitors to scroll down the long page to view the news and events. Instead, you want to provide quick navigation to each section of the page. In addition, you want the visitors to be able to directly navigate to the "Events" section in the newsandevents.html file from the "Our Company" page.

---

1. Create named anchors in the newsandevents.html file.

    a. Click at the end of the heading "July 30, 2009."

    b. In the **INSERT** panel, click **Named Anchor.**

    c. In the **Named Anchor** dialog box, in the **Anchor name** text box, type *july09* and click **OK.**

    d. In the document window, click outside the inserted named anchor.

    e. In the document window, observe that an anchor marker appears at the end of the "July 30, 2009" heading indicating that a named anchor has been created.

    July 30, 2009

    f. Create an anchor named *aug09* for the heading "August 12, 2009," an anchor named *nov09* for the heading "Nov 14, 2009," and another anchor named *events* for the heading "Events."

    g. Scroll up and click at the end of the heading "News and Events."

    h. In the **INSERT** panel, click **Named Anchor.**

    i. In the **Named Anchor** dialog box, in the **Anchor name** text box, type *top* and click **OK.**

---

2. Create links for the anchors.

    a. Under the heading "News and Events," click at the beginning of the text "July 30, 2009."

b.   On the status bar, click **<li>** to select the line.

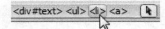

c.   In the **PROPERTIES** panel, click in the **Link** text box, type ***#july09*** and then press **Enter.**

d.   Create an anchor link for the item "August 12, 2009" to the named anchor "aug09," an anchor link for the item "November 14, 2009" to the named anchor "nov09," and another anchor link for the item "Events" to the named anchor "events."

e.   In the document window, scroll down and under the heading "July 30, 2009," select the text **"Back to Top."**

f.   In the **PROPERTIES** panel, click in the **Link** text box, type ***#top*** and then press **Enter.**

g.   Under each heading, create anchor links for the text "Back to Top" to the named anchor "top."

h.   Switch to Code view.

i.   On line **125,** observe the anchor name specified in the "name" attribute of the <a> tag, and on line **131,** observe the "href" attribute specified in the <a> tag, indicating that the text "Back to Top" is linked to the anchor "top."

3.   Preview the web page in a browser.

a.   Save the file.

b.   On the **Document** toolbar, click the **Preview/Debug in browser** button and choose **Preview in IExplore.**

c.   If necessary, in the **Information Bar** message box, click **OK.**

d.   Click the **Events** link to move to the **Events** section.

e.   Click the **Back to Top** link to move to the top of the page.

f.   Close the Internet Explorer window.

g.   Close the file.

4.   Create a link to the **Events** section in the newsandevents.html file.

a.   In the **FILES** panel, double-click **ourcompany.html** to open it.

b.   Switch to Design view.

c.   Scroll down to the bottom of the page.

d.   Above the library item, click at the beginning of the word "Click," hold down **Shift,** and click after the word "here" to select the text "Click here."

e.   In the **PROPERTIES** panel, click in the **Link** text box, type ***newsandevents.html#events*** and then press **Enter.**

f.   Save the file.

g.   On the **Document** toolbar, click the **Preview/Debug in browser** button and choose **Preview in IExplore.**

h.   Scroll down and click the **Click here** link to view the **Events** section of the newsandevents.html file.

i.   If necessary, in the **Information Bar** message box, click **OK.**

j.   Close the Internet Explorer window.

k.   Close the ourcompany.html file.

TOPIC C
Create Email Links

You created hyperlinks. Now, you will enable site visitors to send email by accessing their email application directly from the web page. In this topic, you will create email links.

Visitors to your website will often look for ways to contact you through email. By providing email links, you can enable visitors to quickly send email to request information or provide their suggestions and feedback on your site.

Email Link

An email link added to a website enables visitors to quickly open their default email application from a web page. The address of the person who should be contacted for queries or feedback is automatically filled in. Email links can be created for both text and images.

Email Clients

If you have email clients such as Microsoft Outlook, Outlook Express, or Windows Mail installed on your system, when you click an email link it will automatically open the default email client. If you have an email account from a free email service provider, you need to have the email address configured in the email client to be able to send and receive email. Email addresses, used in email links on site pages, may be gathered by web crawlers for the purposes of establishing spam victims.

How to Create Email Links

Procedure Reference: Create an Email Link

To create an email link:

1. Select the desired text or image.
2. Create an email link.

    ● In the **PROPERTIES** panel, click **HTML** and in the **Link** text box, click and type *mailto:* followed by the email address to be linked or;

     Do not leave any space between the text "mailto:" and the email address.

    ● Create an email link using the **Email Link** dialog box.
    a. In the **INSERT** panel, click **Email Link.**
    b. If necessary, in the **Email Link** dialog box, in the **Text** text box, type the desired text.
    c. In the **E-Mail** text box, type the email address and click **OK.**
3. If necessary, verify the email link in a browser.
    a. Preview the web page in a browser.
    b. Click the email link to open the email application with the email address of the contact person filled in automatically.
    c. Close the email application and the browser window.

ACTIVITY 5-3
Creating an Email Link

Data Files:

career.html

Before You Begin:

1. Ensure that you have an email account configured in the email client installed on your computer.

2. In the **FILES** panel, double-click the career.html to open it.

Scenario:

You want site visitors to be able to post their queries or send feedback about the website to the site administrator.

---

1. Create an email link.

   a. In the document window, scroll down to the bottom of the page.

   b. Above the heading "Our Email IDs," click after the comma in the sentence and press the **Spacebar.**

   c. In the **INSERT** panel, click **Email Link** to open the **Email Link** dialog box.

   d. In the **Text** text box, type *contact us*

   e. In the **Email** text box, click and type *careers@ourglobalcompany.com*

   f. Click **OK** to create the email hyperlink.

   g. Save the file.

---

2. Verify the email link.

   a. On the **Document** toolbar, click the **Preview/Debug in browser** button and choose **Preview in IExplore.**

   b. Click the **contact us** email link to open the email application.

   c. In the **New Message** window, in the **To** text box, observe that the email address is filled in automatically.

   d. Close the **New Message** window.

   e. In the **Microsoft Office Outlook** message box, click **NO.**

   f. Close the Internet Explorer window.

---

3. **True or False? Email links can be created only for text.**

___ True

___ False

TOPIC D
Create Image Maps

You created email links. You can also link a section of an image to a web page. In this topic, you will create image maps.

Assume that you have an image on the home page depicting the various services provided by your company. Instead of providing text hyperlinks to all the pages on the site, you can represent the links graphically in a single image and turn selected regions of the image to act as links.

Hotspots

A *hotspot* is an area on an image that can be clicked to open a linked web page. Hotspots can be rectangular, oval, or polygonal. You can create a hotspot using the hotspot tools in the **PROPERTIES** panel.

Figure 5-2: Display of hotspot areas on the document page and the hotspot tool.

Overlapping Hotspots

You can create two or more overlapping hotspots on an image map. The ones you draw first appear first in the HTML code and take precedence over the ones below them. For example, if you create a large hotspot and then a smaller one that fits into the large one, clicking anywhere within the hotspot, even on the smaller one, will jump to the large hotspot's link. This is because the large hotspot, having been created first, takes precedence over the smaller one. You can work with hotspots as you intend by either reordering the lines of HTML for each hotspot or using the **Bring To Front** or **Send To Back** menu command.

Hotspot Shapes

Dreamweaver generates code automatically when hotspot tools for different shapes are used to create hotspots.

The following table describes the code.

Shape	Code
Rectangle	`<area shape="rect" coords="71,38,366,77" href="index.html" alt="Home" />`
Circle	`<area shape="circle" coords="35,53,24" href="clients.html" alt="Clients" />`
Polygon	`<area shape="poly" coords="422,78,424,27,629,15,657,79" href="contact.html" alt="Contact Us" />`

Image Maps

An *image map* is a single image that contains one or more hotspots. These hotspots can be used to link different regions of the image to different web pages rather than splitting the image to be linked to different pages.

Best Practices to Create Image Maps

Image maps require the usage of large images so that different regions of the image may be linked to different pages. The use of large images increases the download time for pages that use image maps. To reduce the file size of such images, it is recommended that you use images without too much detail and with a limited number of colors. It is also important to use images in a format that will reduce the file size of the image. Unlike text links, image maps often do not provide users with information of what to expect on the linked page. You can provide this information using the `alt` and `title` attributes.

How to Create Image Maps

Procedure Reference: Create an Image Map

To create an image map:

1. Select an image.
2. In the **PROPERTIES** panel, in the **Map** section, select the desired hotspot tool.
3. Place the mouse pointer at the desired location and drag to create a hotspot.
4. In the **Dreamweaver** message box, click **OK.**
5. In the **PROPERTIES** panel, in the **Map** text box, type a unique name for the image map.
6. In the **PROPERTIES** panel, in the **Alt** text box, type alternate text for the hotspot.

 The alternate text for hotspots is used by software that reads web pages aloud. This is very helpful for visually impaired people who use screen readers. In regular browsers, when a user hovers the mouse pointer over an image hotspot, the alternate text of the hotspot, not the image, is displayed.

7. Link the hotspot to the desired web page using the **PROPERTIES** panel.
8. If necessary, create other hotspots and link them to the pages.

9. If necessary, resize the hotspot section.

    a. In the **PROPERTIES** panel, click the **Pointer Hotspot** tool.

    b. On the image, click the desired hotspot section and drag its handle to move or resize the selected hotspot section.

10. If necessary, verify the hotspot links in a browser.

    a. Preview the web page in a browser.

    b. Click the hotspots on the image map to view the respective pages.

    c. Close the browser window.

ACTIVITY 5-4
Creating Image Maps

Data Files:

career.html

Before You Begin:

The career.html file is open.

Scenario:

The career.html page contains a banner image of your website with a logo and the company name. You want users to be able to access the home page of your site if they click a specific region on the image.

---

1.   Create hotspots on the image.

   a.   In the document window, scroll up and select the banner at the top of the page.

   b.   In the **PROPERTIES** panel, in the **Map** section, select the **Rectangular Hotspot** tool. 🔲

   c.   In the selected image, click and drag from the upper-left corner of the text "Our Global Company" to the bottom-right corner of the text to create a rectangle over "Our Global Company."

   d.   In the **Dreamweaver** message box, click **OK.**

   e.   In the **PROPERTIES** panel, click in the **Alt** text box, type *Home* and press **Enter** to set the alternate text of the hotspot.

   f.   In the **PROPERTIES** panel, in the **Map** section, select the **Circle Hotspot** tool. ⭕

   g.   In the selected image, click and drag from the upper-left corner near the circular logo to the bottom-right corner to cover the circular logo in the image.

   h.   In the **Dreamweaver** message box, click **OK.**

   i.   In the **PROPERTIES** panel, click in the **Alt** text box, type *Home* and press **Enter** to set the alternate text of the hotspot.

---

2.   Link the hotspots to the index.html page.

   a.   In the **PROPERTIES** panel, in the **Map** section, select the **Pointer Hotspot** tool. ▲

   b.   Select the rectangular hotspot.

   c.   In the **PROPERTIES** panel, double-click in the **Link** text box, type *index.html* and press **Enter** to link the hotspot.

   d.   Select the circular hotspot.

e. In the **PROPERTIES** panel, double-click in the **Link** text box, type ***index.html*** and press **Enter** to link the hotspot.

3. Preview the web page in a browser.

   a. Save the file.

   b. On the **Document** toolbar, click the **Preview/Debug in browser** button and choose **Preview in IExplore.**

   c. Click the text **"Our Global Company"** in the image to view the home page.

   d. Click **Back.**

   e. Click the logo in the image to view the home page.

   f. Close the Internet Explorer window.

   g. Close the file.

TOPIC E
Create Image Link Rollovers

An effective user-navigation interface goes a long way in enhancing visitors' experience. The simplest method for creating a user-navigation interface is by using rollovers. In this topic, you will create rollovers.

You can grab the attention of users to your site by making it visually appealing and user friendly. One navigation method that handles this effectively is that of rollovers.

Rollovers

A **rollover** is an element on a web page that provides visual feedback and facilitates web page navigation. A rollover consists of several image states, each of which corresponds to the type of action of the mouse pointer over the image. The most common image states are the up, over, and down states. Rollovers usually contain images that vary slightly from the original, giving subtle feedback on the position of the mouse pointer.

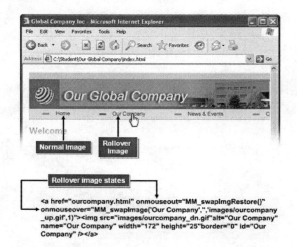

Figure 5-3: Rollover images on a document page.

 JavaScript is used most commonly to switch between image states. Advanced CSS techniques can also be used to achieve the same rollover effect.

The Rollover Image Button

The **Rollover Image** button in the **INSERT** panel allows you to create simple rollovers without having to specify the `onMouseOver` and `onMouseOut` events manually. You can also add more events using the options available on the **Behaviors** tab of the **TAG INSPECTOR** panel.

Using Assets Created in Adobe® Fireworks®

Assets created in Adobe Fireworks are extensively used while creating web pages. Assets saved in Adobe Fireworks can be used on web pages to create image links, as rollover images, and on navigation bars. Adobe Fireworks can also be used to create buttons and navigation bars that can be inserted into web pages in Dreamweaver.

How to Create Image Link Rollovers

Procedure Reference: Create Rollovers

To create rollovers:

1. If necessary, select the existing image for which a rollover needs to be created, and delete it.

2. Display the **Insert Rollover Image** dialog box.
    *   Choose **Insert→Image Objects→Rollover Image** or;
    *   In the **INSERT** panel, click **Image** and select **Rollover Image.**

3. In the **Image name** text box, type a name for the rollover.

4. Next to the **Original Image** text box, click **Browse,** navigate to the folder containing the image, select the image, and click **OK.**

5. Next to the **Rollover Image** text box, click **Browse,** navigate to the folder containing the image, select the image, and click **OK.**

6. If necessary, check the **Preload rollover image** check box to load images in advance and to prevent delay during the image rollover change.

7. In the **Alternate text** text box, type a name for the rollover.

8. Specify a path to the HTML file which you want to open on clicking the rollover.
    *   In the **When clicked, Go to URL** text box, type the path.
    *   Next to the **When clicked, Go to URL** text box, click **Browse,** navigate to the desired folder, select the file, and click **OK.**

9. Click **OK** to close the **Insert Rollover Image** dialog box.

10. Save and preview the web page in a browser.

ACTIVITY 5-5
Creating Image Link Rollovers

Data Files:

index.html

Setup:

In the **FILES** panel, double-click index.html to open it.

Scenario:

You have a list of various links on the main page. Now, you want to replace the images of these links and link each image to its corresponding details on a separate web page. While you want the work involved to be simple, you also need to ensure that it makes your pages interactive.

---

1. Display the **Insert Rollover Image** dialog box.

    a. Below the banner image, select the **Home** image.

    b. Delete the image.

    c. Choose **Insert→Image Objects→Rollover Image** to display the **Insert Rollover Image** dialog box.

---

2. Create a rollover effect with images for the Home link.

    a. In the **Image name** text box, type *Home*

    b. Next to the **Original image** text box, click **Browse** to display the **Original Image** dialog box.

    c. If necessary, navigate to the C:\084502Data\Working with Links\Our Global Company\ images folder.

    d. Select **home_up.gif** and click **OK**.

    e. Next to the **Rollover image** text box, click **Browse** to display the **Rollover Image** dialog box.

    f. Select **home_down.gif** and click **OK**.

---

3. Set the **Home** image as a link.

    a. In the **Insert Rollover Image** dialog box, verify that the **Preload rollover image** check box is checked.

    b. In the **Alternate text** text box, click and type *Home*

    c. In the **When clicked, Go to URL** text box, click and type *index.html*

    d. Click **OK** to close the **Insert Rollover Image** dialog box.

---

4. Create rollover effects for the other images.

    a. Delete the **Our Company** image.

    b. Use the images **ourcompany_up.gif** and **ourcompany_down.gif** to create a rollover effect for the **Our Company** image with the name *Our Company* and alternate text *Our Company* and link it to the ourcompany.html web page.

    c. Delete the **News & Events** image.

    d. Use the images **news_up.gif** and **news_down.gif** to create a rollover effect for the **News & Events** image with the name *News & Events* and alternate text *News & Events* and link it to the newsandevents.html web page.

    e. Delete the **Clients & Partners** image.

    f. Use the images **clients_up.gif** and **clients_down.gif** to create a rollover effect for the **Clients & Partners** image with the name *Clients & Partners* and alternate text *Clients & Partners* and link it to the clients.html web page.

    g. In the document window, scroll to the right and delete the **Career** image.

    h. Use the images **career_up.gif** and **career_down.gif** to create a rollover effect for the **Career** image with the name *Career* and alternate text *Career* and link it to the career.html web page.

    i. Save the file.

5. Preview the page in a browser.

    a. On the **Document** toolbar, click the **Preview/Debug in browser** button and choose **Preview in IExplore.**

    b. In the **Information Bar** message box, check the **Don't show me this message again** check box and click **OK.**

    c. Click the **Information** bar and choose **Allow Blocked Content.**

    d. In the **Security Warning** message box, click **Yes.**

    e. Move the mouse pointer over the **Our Company** image to observe the rollover effect.

    f. Click the **Our Company** image to view the linked page.

    g. Close the Internet Explorer window.

    h. Close the index.html file.

Lesson 5 Follow-up

In this lesson, you created text links and image links. You also created image maps and anchors. Links aid visitors in navigating through a site and accessing web pages quickly.

1. **What might prompt you to create image links for your website?**

2. **Which links do you anticipate you might want to add to all web pages on a site? Why?**

6 | Uploading a Website

Lesson Time: 50 minutes

Lesson Objectives:

In this lesson, you will upload a website.

You will:

● Validate a website.

● Upload files onto a site.

Introduction

You connected the web pages that constitute a website, and now you want to make it accessible to the target audience. In this lesson, you will upload a website.

People with different abilities and varied systems will access the information on your website. You need to ensure that the information on the web pages is accessible to all as intended. By validating content and uploading it, you can achieve this.

This lesson covers all or part of the following Adobe Web Communication using Dreamweaver CS5 objectives:

● Topic A

■ Objective 1.4a: Define website accessibility

■ Objective 1.4b: Demonstrate knowledge of W3C Priority 1 Checkpoints and the W3C Priority 2 POUR principles for making a website accessible

■ Objective 1.4c: Explain why including accessibility in website design matters to clients and the target audience

■ Objective 1.4d: Identify elements of an HTML page that can be read by screen readers

■ Objective 2.2a: Identify website elements that display differently on various operating systems and browser versions/configurations

■ Objective 2.2b: Demonstrate knowledge of page elements that may not appear the same in different browsers

■ Objective 2.2c: Demonstrate knowledge of BrowserLab online service for cross-browser compatibility testing.

■ Objective 2.4c: Identify specific techniques used to make a website accessible to viewers with visual and motor impairments

- Objective 2.4d: Identify elements of a website that by default are not read by screen readers
- Objective 5.2i: Demonstrate knowledge of how to define, modify, and check CSS rules

- Topic B
  - Objective 6.1b: Demonstrate knowledge of how to test links by using the Check Links Sitewide command
  - Objective 6.5a: Demonstrate knowledge of how to delete files by using the Files panel
  - Objective 6.5b: Demonstrate knowledge of how to rename files and update links by using the Files panel
  - Objective 6.5d: Demonstrate knowledge of the terms "Get," "Put," "Check In," "Check Out," "Publish," and "Remote Server" as they apply to managing files and publishing a website
  - Objective 6.5e: Demonstrate knowledge of expanding and collapsing the Files panel to access features such as the site map, get and put, check in and out, and refreshing the Files panel
  - Objective 6.6a: Demonstrate knowledge of how to set up a connection to a remote server
  - Objective 6.6b: Demonstrate knowledge of how to publish files to a remote server
  - Objective 6.6c: Demonstrate knowledge of how to use the Files panel to connect to and disconnect from a remote site, how to upload files to a remote site, and how to download files from a remote site.

TOPIC A

Validate a Website

You created the required web pages for your website and are ready to upload the files onto the site. However, before uploading, you need to check the web pages for proper functioning, so that visitors of the website do not encounter problems. In this topic, you will validate a website.

Your website will reach a varied audience when more users access it. Validating your web pages and checking the website for compliance with accessibility standards will help you ensure that it is accessible to everyone.

Accessibility Standards

Website accessibility refers to the process of enabling people with visual, motor, auditory, and other disabilities to access web pages. To ensure web accessibility, web developers need to check that the web pages they develop adhere to accessibility standards. Significant accessibility standards are Section 508 of the Federal Rehabilitation Act and the World Wide Web Consortium Web Accessibility Initiative.

Section 508 Standards

Section 508 of the Federal Rehabilitation Act states that federal agencies should ensure that employees as well as people with disabilities are able to access technology. Section 508 standards for web accessibility are defined as follows:

§1194.22 Web-based intranet and Internet information and applications:

a. A text equivalent for every non-text element shall be provided (e.g., using "alt" or "longdesc" in element content).

b. Equivalent alternatives for any multimedia presentation shall be synchronized with the presentation.

c. Web pages shall be designed so that all information conveyed with color is also available without color, for example from context or markup.

d. Documents shall be organized so that they are readable, without requiring an associated style sheet.

e. Redundant text links shall be provided for each active region of a server-side image map.

f. Client-side image maps shall be provided instead of server-side image maps, except where the regions cannot be defined with an available geometric shape.

g. Row and column headers shall be identified for data tables.

h. Markup shall be used to associate data cells and header cells for data tables that have two or more logical levels of row or column headers.

i. Frames shall be titled with text that facilitates frame identification and navigation.

j. Pages shall be designed to avoid causing the screen to flicker with a frequency greater than 2 Hz and lower than 55 Hz.

k. A text-only page, with equivalent information or functionality, shall be provided to make a website comply with the provisions of this part, when compliance cannot be accomplished in any other way. The content of the text-only page shall be updated whenever the primary page changes.

l.   When pages utilize scripting languages to display content or to create interface elements, the information provided by the script shall be identified with functional text that can be read by assistive technology.

m.   When a web page requires an applet, plug-in, or other application be present on the client system to interpret page content, the page must provide a link to the plug-in or applet that complies with §1194.21(a) through (l) of Section 508 Technical Standards.

n.   When electronic forms are designed to be completed online, the form shall allow people using assistive technology, to access the information, field elements, and functionality required for completion and submission of the form, including all directions and cues.

o.   A method that permits users to skip repetitive navigation links shall be provided.

p.   When a timed response is required, the user shall be alerted and given sufficient time to indicate that more time is required.

The Board interprets paragraphs (a) through (k) of this section as consistent with the following priority 1 Checkpoints of the Web Content Accessibility Guidelines 1.0 (WCAG 1.0) (May 5, 1999) published by the Web Accessibility Initiative of the World Wide Web Consortium.

Here are the corresponding section 1194.22 paragraphs and WCAG 1.0 checkpoints: (a): 1.1, (b): 1.4, (c): 2.1, (d): 6.1, (e): 1.2, (f): 9.1, (g): 5.1, (h): 5.2, (i): 12.1, (j): 7.1, (k): 11.4.

Paragraphs (l), (m), (n), (o), and (p) of this section are different from WCAG 1.0. Web pages that conform to WCAG 1.0, level A (i.e., all priority 1 checkpoints) must also meet the requirements of paragraphs (l), (m), (n), (o), and (p) of this section to comply with this section. WCAG 1.0 is available at **http://www.w3.org/TR/ WAI-WEBCONTENT/.**

Improving Accessibility of a Website

Web content can be delivered with robust accessibility features. The following are a few techniques to improve accessibility of rich media content for viewers with different disabilities:

● Auditory impairment: Provide captions for any audio that is used.

● Vision impairment:

■ Use elements with a lot of contrast in color.

■ Allow scaling of content.

■ Ensure accessibility of elements through screen readers.

● Motor impairment:

■ Ensure keyboard accessibility as an alternate to other input devices.

■ Avoid usage of interaction that requires fine motor skills.

■ Provide easy navigation structures.

Supporting International Languages

The attribute lang = language-code [CI] specifies the base language of text content and also an element's attribute values. The default value of this particular attribute is not known. A user agent may use the language information that is specified using the lang attribute to control rendering in different ways.

W3C Standards (HTML Validation)

There are some important validation methods that should be followed to ensure that users do not encounter any problems while accessing a website. You must use the automated accessibility and browser validation tools, and validate syntax and style sheets. You need to use a text-only browser or emulator and multiple graphic browsers in various settings, such as with sounds and graphics loaded, graphics not loaded, sounds not loaded, no mouse, frames, scripts, style sheets, and applets not loaded to validate a page. In addition, you can use several browsers, old and new, and also self-voicing browsers, screen readers, magnification software, or a small display to perform the validation. You must also use spelling and grammar checkers and must review the document for clarity and simplicity. Alternatively, you can request people with disabilities to review the documents.

W3C Deprecated Tags

When new constructs are being used, certain elements or attributes become outdated. These are called deprecated elements or attributes. The reference manual of W3C defines deprecated elements in appropriate locations and also clearly marks them as deprecated. For backward compatibility, user agents should continue to support deprecated elements. For example, <applet>, <basefont>, <center>, <dir>, <font>, <isindex>, <menu>, <s>, <strike>, and <u> are deprecated tags in the HTML 4.01 specification.

WCAG Priority 1 Checklist

The Web Accessibility Initiative of the World Wide Web Consortium has developed access guidelines that are included in Section 508, and a website should contain elements, such as Alt text or verbal tags, to make it easier for the user to access the web pages. For example, people with sight disabilities can rely on screen readers, which translate the on-screen objects into audible output, and also on Braille displays. The elements of the WCAG Priority 1 checklist are as follows:

- Provide a text equivalent for every non-text element (for example, "alt", "longdesc" or using a linked document). This includes: images, graphical representations of text (including symbols), image map regions, animations (e.g., animated GIFs), applets and programmatic objects, ASCII art, frames, scripts, images used as list bullets, spacers, graphical buttons, sounds (played with or without user interaction), standalone audio files, audio tracks of video, and video.

- Ensure that all information conveyed with color is also available without color for example, from context or markup.

- Clearly identify changes in the natural language of a document's text and any text equivalents (for example, captions).

- Organize documents so they may be read without style sheets. For example, when an HTML document is rendered without associated style sheets, it must still be possible to read the document.

- Ensure that equivalents for dynamic content are updated when the dynamic content changes.

- Until user agents allow users to control flickering, avoid causing the screen to flicker.

- Use the clearest and simplest language appropriate for a site's content.

- Provide redundant text links for each active region of a server-side image map.

- Provide client-side image maps instead of server-side image maps, except where the regions cannot be defined with an available geometric shape.

- For data tables, identify row and column headers.

- For data tables that have two or more logical levels of row or column headers, use markup to associate data cells and header cells.
- Title each frame to facilitate frame identification and navigation.
- Ensure that pages are usable when scripts, applets, or other programmatic objects are turned off or not supported. If this is not possible, provide equivalent information on an alternative accessible page.
- Until user agents can automatically read aloud the text equivalent of a visual track, provide an auditory description of the important information of the visual track of a multimedia presentation.
- For any time-based multimedia presentation (for example, a movie or animation), synchronize equivalent alternatives (for example, captions or auditory descriptions of the visual track) with the presentation.
- If, after best efforts, you cannot create an accessible page, provide a link to an alternative page that uses W3C technologies, is accessible, has equivalent information (or functionality), and is updated as often as the inaccessible (original) page.

 The alternate text in images is used by software that reads web pages aloud. If there is no alternate text, then the software reads the file name. Specifying alternate text for every image on your site will help ensure compliance with Section 508 for accessibility.

WCAG Priority 2 Checklist

The elements of the WCAG Priority 2 checklist are as follows:

- Ensure that foreground and background color combinations provide sufficient contrast when viewed by someone with color defects or when viewed on a black and white screen. (Priority 2 for images, Priority 3 for text.)
- Use markup rather than images to convey information when an appropriate markup language exists.
- Create documents that validate to published formal grammar.
- Use style sheets to control layout and presentation.
- Use relative rather than absolute units in markup language attribute values and style sheet property values.
- Use header elements to convey document structure and use them according to specification.
- Mark up lists and list items properly.
- Mark up quotations. Do not use quotation markup for formatting effects such as indentation.
- Ensure that dynamic content is accessible or provide an alternative presentation or page.
- Until user agents allow users to control blinking, avoid causing content to blink (that is, change the presentation at a regular rate, such as turning on and off).
- Until user agents provide the ability to stop the refresh, do not create periodically auto-refreshing pages.
- Until user agents provide the ability to stop auto-redirect, do not use markup to redirect pages automatically. Instead, configure the server to perform redirects.

- Until user agents allow users to turn off spawned windows, do not cause pop-ups or other windows to appear and do not change the current window without informing the user.

- Use W3C technologies when they are available and appropriate for a task, and use the latest versions when supported.

- Avoid deprecated features of W3C technologies.

- Divide large blocks of information into more manageable groups where natural and appropriate.

- Clearly identify the target of each link.

- Provide metadata to add semantic information to pages and sites.

- Provide information about the general layout of a site (for example, a site map or table of contents).

- Use navigation mechanisms in a consistent manner.

- Do not use tables for layouts unless the table makes sense when linearized. Otherwise, if the table does not make sense, provide an alternative equivalent (which may be a linearized version).

- If a table is used for layouts, do not use any structural markup for the purpose of visual formatting.

- Describe the purpose of frames and how frames relate to each other if it is not obvious by frame titles alone.

- Until user agents support explicit associations between labels and form controls, for all form controls with implicitly associated labels, ensure that the label is properly positioned.

- Associate labels explicitly with their controls.

- For scripts and applets, ensure that event handlers are input device-independent.

- Until user agents allow users to freeze moving content, avoid movement in pages.

- Make programmatic elements such as scripts and applets directly accessible or compatible with assistive technologies. (Priority 1 if functionality is important and not presented elsewhere, otherwise Priority 2.)

- Ensure that any element that has its own interface can be operated in a device-independent manner.

- For scripts, specify logical event handlers rather than device-dependent event handlers.

Screen Readers

A screen reader is a software application that interprets content displayed on a monitor. The interpreted text is presented to users in a different output form such as spoken audio or Braille output. Screen readers are extensively used by visually impaired persons. The content on a website is made accessible to the visually impaired audience by incorporating accessibility features that facilitate the use of screen readers.

Though screen readers interpret content that is displayed on the monitor, there are a number of elements that they cannot interpret. Images, rich media, and forms and their elements are interpreted with their `alt` attribute value. Colors used for text and background are not interpreted. Though text headings that use the `<h1>` to `<h6>` tags are interpreted, other text formatting tags such as `<strong>` and `<em>` are not interpreted. Tables and their elements are read, but nested tables are not recognized by screen readers.

The Results Panel Group

The *Results panel group* contains tools that you can use to search for information on a website and set preferences for validation of a website and of browser compatibility issues. These tools are grouped into different panels based on their functionality. The following table describes the various options in the different panels.

Panel	Description
SEARCH	Allows you to find and replace text on web pages.
REFERENCE	Provides reference information about different languages and elements you might use.
VALIDATION	Allows you to check the code on a web page. Dreamweaver can validate web pages in many languages.
BROWSER COMPATIBILITY	Checks the browser compatibility of the various elements used on a web page.
LINK CHECKER	Lists external links, broken links, and orphaned files that you may want to identify and delete.
SITE REPORTS	Allows you to generate workflow and HTML reports.
FTP LOG	Allows you to view all FTP file transfer activities.
SERVER DEBUG	Provides information on how to debug a ColdFusion application.

 Files that are created, but not referenced on the website are referred to as orphaned files.

Adobe CSS Advisor

Adobe CSS Advisor is a website that provides information, suggestions, and tips on the latest browser and code issues in Dreamweaver. If a browser compatibility issue is found on the web pages that you have developed, a link is provided in the **BROWSER COMPATIBILITY** panel of the **Results** panel group. Accessing this link will enable you to read the documentation about the issue on the *Adobe CSS Advisor* website. In addition to referring information on the **Adobe CSS Advisor** website, you can post your comments and suggestions. You can also add new issues.

Web Page Rendering on Different Browsers

Often web pages display differently on different web browsers. This is because browsers interpret HTML and CSS code using different standards. Browsers also render pages differently because the default values for attributes of HTML tags and CSS properties vary for different browsers.

Common elements that display differently on browsers are lists, text links, form elements, moving text, blinking text, and text formatting. CSS properties that cause web pages to render differently include borders, padding, and margins. These properties are applied to elements such as tables, div containers, and images.

Validator Preferences

Using the *validator preferences,* you can specify the tag libraries that you want to check code against. You can also specify the exact problems that need to be checked and the messages that are to be displayed.

Site Reports

The **Reports** dialog box allows you to generate reports for a site, classified under two categories, namely, **Workflow** and **HTML Reports. Workflow** reports help improve collaboration among team members. **HTML Reports** validate a website for missing alternate text, untitled documents, and other tag-related issues that help optimize code. The site reports are displayed in the **SITE REPORTS** panel of the **Results** panel group.

Adobe BrowserLab

Adobe BrowserLab allows you to preview web pages within Dreamweaver, without posting them to a publicly-accessible server first. Adobe BrowserLab is one of the CS Live online services, allowing you to preview files from your local Dreamweaver site, or from a remote or testing server.

How to Validate a Website

Procedure Reference: Set Validator Preferences

To set validator preferences:

1. Open the **Preferences** dialog box.
    - Choose **Edit→Preferences** or;
    - In the **Results** panel group, select the **VALIDATION** panel, click the **Validate** button, and choose **Settings.**
2. In the left pane, select **Validator.**
3. In the **Validator** section, specify the desired options.

 You can choose only one version of each language to validate against.

4. If necessary, change the validator options.
    a. In the **Validator** section, click **Options.**
    b. In the **Validator Options** dialog box, in the **Display** section, uncheck the options you do not need.
    c. In the **Check for** section, uncheck the options you do not need.
    d. Click **OK** to save the changes to the validator options.
5. In the **Preferences** dialog box, click **OK** to save the preferences.

Procedure Reference: Check Target Browsers

To check target browsers:

1. Open the desired file.

2. Choose **Window→Results→Browser Compatibility** to display the **BROWSER COM-PATIBILITY** panel in the **Results** panel group.

3. If necessary, change the target browser settings.

    a. Click the **Check Browser Compatibility** button and choose **Settings.**

    b. In the **Target Browsers** dialog box, in the **Minimum browser versions** section, check the check boxes of the required browsers, and from the drop-down list next to each selected browser, select the required version.

    c. Click **OK** to save the settings.

4. Check the target browser for the current document.

    ● Choose **File→Check Page→Browser Compatibility** or;

    ● In the **Results** panel group, in the **BROWSER COMPATIBILITY** panel, click the **Check Browser Compatibility** button and choose **Check Browser Compatibility.**

5. If necessary, in the **BROWSER COMPATIBILITY** panel, identify the issues listed.

6. If necessary, correct the browser compatibility issues on the web page.

7. If necessary, in the **BROWSER COMPATIBILITY** panel, click the **Save Report** button and save the report.

8. If necessary, in the **BROWSER COMPATIBILITY** panel, click the **Browse Report** button to view the report in the browser window.

9. Save the file.

Procedure Reference: Generate Site Reports

To generate site reports:

1. In the **FILES** panel, double-click a file to open it.

2. Choose **Window→Results→Site Reports** to display the **SITE REPORTS** panel in the **Results** panel group.

3. Open the **Reports** dialog box.

    ● In the **SITE REPORTS** panel, click the **Reports** button or;

    ● From the **FILES** panel options menu, choose **Site→Reports.**

4. In the **Reports** dialog box, in the **Select reports** section, check the desired check boxes.

    ● Below the **Workflow Reports** sub-tree, check the desired check boxes.

    ● Below the **HTML Reports** sub-tree, check the desired check boxes.

5. In the **Reports** dialog box, from the **Report on** drop-down list, select the desired option.

6. Click **Run.**

7. In the **Results** panel group, in the **SITE REPORTS** panel, in the **File** column, identify the files that contain errors and then in the **Description** column, read through the error description.

8. If necessary, correct the errors on the web pages.

9. If necessary, in the **SITE REPORTS** panel, click **Save Report** to save the report.

10. Save the file.

ACTIVITY 6-1
Ensuring Accessibility Standards

Data Files:

newsandevents.html, index.html

1. If the Our Global Company site was previously defined in Dreamweaver, you must modify the Local Root folder and Default images folder in the site definition so that it is based on the new data from the C:\084502Data\Uploading a Website\Our Global Company folder.

2. In the **FILES** panel, expand the Site - Our Global Company folder.

3. Double-click the **newsandevents.html** file to open it.

Before You Begin:

Scenario:

You created the pages for your website and are ready to upload the site. But, before you allow others to access your website, you need to ensure that all the pages on the site function as intended and people with different abilities and different systems are able to access it.

---

1. Check the newsandevents.html page to determine if it adheres to the XHTML 1.0 Transitional standards.

   a. Choose **Window→Results→Validation** to display the **VALIDATION** panel in the **Results** panel group.

   b. Click the **Validate** button.

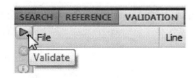

   c. Choose **Settings** to display the **Preferences** dialog box.

   d. Verify that the **Validator** category is selected, and in the **Validator** section, check the **XHTML 1.0 Transitional** check box.

   e. Click **OK.**

---

2. Select the target browsers to check for browser compatibility.

   a. In the **Results** panel group, select the **BROWSER COMPATIBILITY** panel.

b.   Click the **Check Browser Compatibility** button.

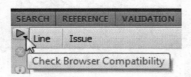

c.   Choose **Settings.**

d.   In the **Target Browsers** dialog box, to the right of the **Firefox** check box, from the drop-down list, select **2.0.**

e.   In the drop-down list to the right of the **Internet Explorer** check box, verify that **6.0** is selected.

f.   Uncheck the **Internet Explorer for Macintosh, Netscape, Opera,** and **Safari** check boxes.

g.   Click **OK** to set the target browsers.

3.   Check the home page for browser compatibility.

a.   In the **FILES** panel, double-click the **index.html** file to open it.

b.   In the **Results** panel group, in the **BROWSER COMPATIBILITY** panel, click the **Check Browser Compatibility** button and choose **Check Browser Compatibility.**

c.   In the **BROWSER COMPATIBILITY** panel, observe that no error messages are displayed.

d.   Close the file.

4.   Generate site reports to show elements that have missing alternate text and failed accessibility standards.

a.   In the **Results** panel group, select the **SITE REPORTS** panel.

b.   Click the **Reports** button.

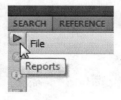

c.   In the **Reports** dialog box, from the **Report on** drop-down list, select **Entire Current Local Site.**

d.   In the **Select reports** section, under the **HTML Reports** sub-tree, check the **Missing Alt Text** check box.

e.   In the **Reports** dialog box, click **Run** to generate the site report.

5.   Generate and save the site report.

a.   In the **Results** panel group, in the **SITE REPORTS** panel, click the **Save Report** button.

    b.   If necessary, in the **Save As** dialog box, navigate to the C:\084502Data\Uploading a Website\Our Global Company folder.

    c.   In the **Save As** dialog box, in the **File name** text box, type *myreport* and click **Save.**

6.   Correct the error displayed in the site report.

    a.   In the **SITE REPORTS** panel, observe the first error displayed with "career.html" in the **File** column and "207" in the **Line** column.

    b.   Double-click the error.

    c.   Switch to Design view.

    d.   In the **PROPERTIES** panel, click in the **Alt** text box, type *Career Page Image of OGC* and press **Enter.**

    e.   In the **Results** panel group, in the **SITE REPORTS** panel, click the **Reports** button.

    f.   In the **Reports** dialog box, in the **Select reports** section, under the **HTML Reports** sub-tree, check the **Missing Alt Text** check box.

    g.   Click **Run** to generate the site report.

    h.   In the **SITE REPORTS** panel, verify that the first error is not displayed.

    i.   Save all the open files.

    j.   Close all the files.

TOPIC B
Upload Files onto a Site

You validated the web pages on your website and ensured that they adhere to accessibility standards. The next step is to upload the files to a remote location so that others can access them. In this topic, you will upload files onto a site.

In an educational institution, a library serves as a central repository for books that students can access. Similarly, a central repository for your website can be a common folder that anyone can access. By uploading the site files to the common folder, you can ensure that your web pages are accessible to everyone.

The Get and Put Commands

The **Get** and **Put** commands allow you to transfer files between a local site and a remote site. The *Get command* allows you to copy files from a remote site to a local site. The *Put command* allows you to upload files from a local site onto a remote site.

 | If errors are encountered during upload or download, Dreamweaver logs them for your review.

Cloaking

Cloaking is an option that allows you to exclude files and folders from site operations such as finding newer versions, transferring files between remote and local sites, and other site wide operations. You can cloak multiple folders and also files of a particular type, but all the files and folders of a site cannot be cloaked at the same time. You can also choose to disable cloaking.

Internet Service Provider

After you build your site, you want to make it available to other users. To do that, you have to transfer them to a web server. If you work with a University, a government agency, or a large company or an organization, you often have a dedicated Internet connection and a web server. If you are an individual or work for a small company, you can use a web hosting service, which provides space on a web server for your use. Additionally, if you have an account with an Internet Service Provider, or ISP, often that account comes with a certain amount of web space. Most web hosting services enable you to use your own domain name (www.[yourcompany].com), whereas ISPs generally do not offer this option. If you publish your site to your ISP, generally the address follows the format www.[ispname].com/[username].

Remote Server Options

The remote server options allow you to specify the access method you want Dreamweaver to use to transfer files between the local and remote folders.

The following table describes the remote server options available.

Remote Server Option	Used To
FTP	Connect to a web server using FTP.

Remote Server Option	Used To
SFTP	Connect to a web server using secure FTP.
Local/Network	Connect to a network folder or computer, functioning as a web server.
WebDAV	Connect to a web server using Web-based Distributed Authoring and Versioning (WebDAV) protocol. The WebDAV protocol allows collaborative editing and managing of files on a web server.
RDS	Connect to a web server using Remote Development Services (RDS). The remote folder must be on a computer running Adobe® ColdFusion®.

Site Upload

If you have an account with an ISP or a web-hosting service, or if you have access to your own web server, you can upload the site to that remote server. In order to successfully transfer the files to the server you are using, you need several main pieces of information such as the account information and the FTP address to access the server. You can also transfer your files to other servers that provide space for hosting your website. An ISP or a web-hosting service will issue a user name and a password associated with your account, and will give you the File Transfer Protocol (FTP) address.

How to Upload Files onto a Site

Procedure Reference: Check the Links on the Site

To check the links on the site:

1. In the **FILES** panel, double-click a file to open it.

2. Choose **Window→Results→Link Checker** to display the **LINK CHECKER** panel in the **Results** panel group.

3. From the **Show** drop-down list, select an option to view broken links, external links, or orphaned files.

4. Check the links for the current document.

   ● Choose **File→Check Page→Links** or;

   ● In the **Results** panel, in the **LINK CHECKER** panel, click the **Check Links** button and choose **Check Links in Current Document.**

5. If necessary, check the links for the entire site.

   ● In the **Results** panel group, in the **LINK CHECKER** panel, click the **Check Links** button and choose **Check Links For Entire Current Local Site.**

   ● In the **FILES** panel, right-click the site root folder and choose **Check Links→Entire Local Site.**

   ● From the **FILES** panel options menu, choose **Site→Check Links Sitewide** or;

   ● Choose **Site→Check Links Sitewide.**

6. If necessary, check the links for multiple files.

    a. In the **FILES** panel, hold down **Ctrl** and select the required files.

    b. Check the links for the selected files.

- In the **Results** panel group, in the **LINK CHECKER** panel, click the **Check Links** button and choose **Check Links For Selected Files in Site** or;

- In the **FILES** panel, right-click the selected files and choose **Check Links→ Selected Files.**

7. If necessary, in the **LINK CHECKER** panel, select a link and correct it.

8. If necessary, in the **LINK CHECKER** panel, click the **Save Report** button to save the report.

9. Save the file.

Procedure Reference: Upload a Site

To upload a site:

1. Open the **Manage Sites** dialog box.

- From the **FILES** panel options menu, choose **Site→Manage Sites.**

- In the **FILES** panel, from the drop-down list at the top-left section of the panel, select **Manage Sites.**

- On the Application bar, click the **Site** button and choose **Manage Sites** or;

- Choose **Site→Manage Sites.**

2. Select the desired site and click **Edit.**

3. In the **Site Definition** dialog box, select the **Advanced** tab and in the **Category** section, select **Remote Info.**

4. In the **Remote Info** section, select an access method to access the files from a remote server and configure it.

- Select FTP as the access method and apply the required settings for configuring it.

    a. From the **Access** drop-down list, select **FTP.**

    b. In the **FTP host** text box, enter the ISP or web-hosting service's FTP address.

    c. If necessary, in the **Host Directory** text box, enter the sub-directory path to place the site files inside a sub-directory within the remote site's root folder.

    d. In the **Login** and **Password** text boxes, enter the login and password assigned by the ISP or web-hosting service.

- Select Local/Network as the access method and apply the required settings for configuring it.

    a. From the **Access** drop-down list, select **Local/Network.**

    b. To the right of the **Remote folder** text box, click the folder icon.

    c. In the **Choose remote root folder for site** dialog box, navigate to the required folder.

    d. If necessary, create a folder.

    e. Open the required remote folder and click **Select.**

- Select WebDAV as the access method and apply the required settings for configuring it.

    a. From the **Access** drop-down list, select **WebDAV.**

b. In the **URL** text box, type the URL of the remote site.

c. In the **Login** and **Password** text boxes, enter the login and password required to access the remote site.

- Select RDS as the access method and apply the required settings for configuring it.

a. From the **Access** drop-down list, select **RDS.**

b. Click **Settings** to display the **Configure RDS Server** dialog box.

c. In the **Host name** text box, type the host name of the remote server.

d. If necessary, in the **Port** text box, type the port number.

e. In the **Username** and **Password** text boxes, enter the user name and password required to access the remote host.

f. Click **OK.**

5. In the **Site Definition** dialog box, click **OK.**

6. In the **Manage Sites** dialog box, click **Done.**

7. In the **FILES** panel, select the root folder of the site.

8. Upload the site files.

- In the **FILES** panel, click the **Put File(s)** button.

- From the **FILES** panel options menu, choose **Site→Put.**

- On the **Document** toolbar, click the **File management** button and choose **Put.**

- Choose **Site→Put.**

9. In the **Dreamweaver** dialog box, click **OK** to upload the entire site to the remote server.

Procedure Reference: Rename a File and Update Links to the File

To rename a file and update links to the file:

1. Rename a file in the **FILES** panel.

a. In the **FILES** panel, select a file in the current site.

b. Rename the file.

- Click the file name.

- Right-click the selected file and choose **Edit→Rename** or;

- From the **FILES** panel options menu, choose **File→Rename.**

c. Type a name for the file.

2. In the **Update Files** dialog box, click **Update** to update all the links to the renamed file.

Procedure Reference: Update Links to a Deleted File

To update links to a deleted file:

1. Delete a file in the **FILES** panel.

a. In the **FILES** panel, select a file in the current site.

b. Delete the file.

- Press **Delete.**

- Right-click the selected file and choose **Edit→Delete** or;

- From the **FILES** panel options menu, choose **File→Delete.**

c. In the **Dreamweaver** message box, click **Yes.**

2.   Change the links to the deleted file on all the site files.

    a.   From the **FILES** panel options menu, choose **Site→Change Link Sitewide.**

    b.   In the **Change Link Sitewide** dialog box, in the **Change all links to** text box, type the name of the deleted file.

    c.   In the **Change Link Sitewide** dialog box, next to the **Into links to** text box, click the folder icon.

    d.   If necessary, in the **Select New Link** dialog box, navigate to a folder.

    e.   Select a file and click **OK.**

    f.   In the **Change Link Sitewide** dialog box, click **OK.**

3.   In the **Update Files** dialog box, click **Update** to update all the links to the renamed file.

Procedure Reference: Update the Site Files

To update the site files:

1.   Update the required files on the local site.

2.   If necessary, change the links on the site.

    a.   From the **FILES** panel options menu, choose **Site→Change Link Sitewide.**

    b.   In the **Change Link Sitewide** dialog box, next to the **Change all links to** text box, click the folder icon.

    c.   If necessary, in the **Select Link to Change** dialog box, navigate to the desired folder.

    d.   Select the desired file and click **OK.**

    e.   In the **Change Link Sitewide** dialog box, next to the **Into links to** text box, click the folder icon.

    f.   If necessary, in the **Select New Link** dialog box, navigate to the desired folder.

    g.   Select the desired file and click **OK.**

    h.   In the **Change Link Sitewide** dialog box, click **OK.**

3.   In the **Update Files** dialog box, click **Update** to update all the links to the renamed file.

4.   From the **FILES** panel options menu, choose **Edit→Select Newer Local** to select the changed files.

5.   Upload the changed files.

    ●   In the **FILES** panel, click the **Put File(s)** button.

    ●   From the **FILES** panel options menu, choose **Site→Put.**

    ●   On the **Document** toolbar, click the **File management** button and choose **Put.**

    ●   Choose **Site→Put.**

6.   In the **Dependent Files - will dismiss in <number of seconds> second(s)** dialog box, click **Yes** to upload the dependent files along with the changed files.

ACTIVITY 6-2
Uploading a Site

Data Files:

newsandevents.html

Scenario:

You finished work on the entire website and thoroughly validated it. For others to view the web pages, you need to place the pages in a location that every user can access.

---

1. Perform the site link check.

   a. In the **Results** panel group, select the **LINK CHECKER** panel.

   b. In the **Results** panel group, in the **LINK CHECKER** panel, in the **Show** drop-down list, verify that **Broken Links** is selected to check for broken links.

   c. Click the **Check Links** button.

   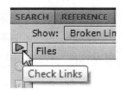

   d. Choose **Check Links For Entire Current Local Site.**

   e. Observe that an error is displayed in the **LINK CHECKER** panel.

   f. Double-click the error message to open the newsandevents.html file.

   g. In the **PROPERTIES** panel, in the **Link** text box, observe that the text "client.html" is selected indicating that the file name is incorrect.

   h. Type *clients.html* and then press **Enter.**

   i. Save the file.

   j. In the **Results** panel group, in the **LINK CHECKER** panel, click the **Check Links** button and choose **Check Links For Entire Current Local Site.**

   k. Verify that no error is displayed in the **LINK CHECKER** panel.

   l. Close the file.

---

2. View external links and orphaned files.

   a. In the **Results** panel group, in the **LINK CHECKER** panel, from the **Show** drop-down list, select **External Links** to view the external files' links.

   b. From the **Show** drop-down list, select **Orphaned Files** to view the files that are not used on your website.

    c.   From the **LINK CHECKER** panel options menu, choose **Close Tab Group** to close the **Results** panel group.

3. Select the remote info access method.

    a.   Choose **Site→Manage Sites** to display the **Manage Sites** dialog box.

    b.   Verify that **Our Global Company** is selected and click **Edit.**

    c.   In the **Site Setup for Our Global Company** dialog box, in the left pane, select the **Servers** category.

    d.   In the right pane, click the **Add new Server** button.

    e.   In the displayed box, in the **Connect using** drop-down list, verify that **FTP** is selected.

4. Specify the FTP server information.

    a.   In the **Server Name** text box, type *OGC*

    b.   In the **FTP Address** text box, type *172.30.4.197* and press **Tab.**

    c.   In the **Username** text box, type *Student* and press **Tab.**

    d.   In the **Password** text box, type *password*

> If a student's ID is 05, then the folder name should be Test_Student05.

    e.   In the **Root Directory** text box, click and type *Test_Student[ID]*

    f.   Verify that the **Save** check box is checked.

    g.   Click **Test** to test the connection to the FTP server.

    h.   In the **Dreamweaver** message box, click **OK.**

    i.   In the displayed dialog box, click **Save.**

    j.   In the **Site Setup for Our Global Company** dialog box, click **Save.**

    k.   In the **Dreamweaver** message box, click **OK.**

    l.   In the **Manage Sites** dialog box, click **Done.**

5. Upload files to the site.

    a.   In the **FILES** panel, verify that the **Site - Our Global Company** folder is selected.

    b.   Click the **Put file(s) to "OGC"** button. 🔼

    c.   In the **Dreamweaver** message box, click **OK** to upload the entire site.

    d.   In the **FILES** panel, click the **Expand to show local and remote sites** button.

    e.   In the left pane, observe that the files on the remote site are displayed.

    f.   Click the **Collapse to show only local or remote site** button.

ACTIVITY 6-3
Uploading Changed Files

Data Files:

career.html

Before You Begin:

In the **FILES** panel, double-click the **career.html** file to open it.

Scenario:

You uploaded your site and then noticed that the heading on the career.html page is misspelled. You need to make the correction on your website.

---

1. Correct the spelling error in the heading on the careers page.

   a. In the heading "Carears," click after the second occurrence of the letter "a."

   b. Press **Backspace** and type *e*

   c. Save the file.

   d. Close the career.html file.

---

2. Upload the modified file to the remote server.

   a. From the **FILES** panel options menu, choose **Edit→Select Newer Local** to select the modified file.

   b. In the **FILES** panel, observe that the career.html file is selected.

   c. In the **FILES** panel, click the **Put file(s) to "OGC"** button to upload the selected file.

   d. In the **Dependent Files - will dismiss in <number of seconds> second(s)** dialog box, click **No** to upload only the career.html file.

   e. Choose **File→Exit** to close the Dreamweaver application.

Lesson 6 Follow-up

In this lesson, you validated your web pages and uploaded them onto a site. This ensures that your website is available on a remote location and users can access it.

1. **Which accessibility standards do you want to ensure that your website meets? Why?**

2. **What do you think is the most important check to be performed before uploading your website? Why?**

Follow-up

In this course, you designed, built, and uploaded a website using the features in the Dreamweaver application. You will now be able to create websites that look appealing and are easily navigable.

1. **How do you think you might customize the Dreamweaver environment to suit your work requirements?**

2. **What are the various page elements that you might use on your web pages?**

3. **What are the various reusable site assets that you might use while developing your website? Why?**

What's Next?

Adobe® Dreamweaver® CS5: Level 2 is the next course in this series.

A | Using Frames

Lesson Time: 30 minutes

Objectives:

In this lesson, you will work with framesets.

You will:

● Create framesets.

Introduction

You uploaded a website and allowed users to access it. The website contains web pages that are displayed one at a time in the browser window. However, at times you may need to display more than one web page in the same browser window. In this lesson, you will work with frames.

When you design a website, you may want to maintain uniformity in the names and links of different parts of the website across all pages. It is tedious to recreate these elements on all web pages. A better option would be to use frames.

TOPIC A
Create Framesets

Using framesets will allow you to lay out your web page to display multiple pages simultaneously. In this topic, you will create a frameset.

As a web designer, your aim is to design web pages that are easy to navigate and to present required information in an organized way. To achieve this goal, you may need to select an appropriate layout mechanism for the web pages you design. Creating framesets will help you lay out web pages in such a way that they are easy to navigate, and present well-organized information.

Frames

Frames are used to lay out a web page by dividing the browser window into multiple regions. Each frame can display a web page that is different from those displayed in the rest of the browser window. Most websites display logos, advertisements, the title of the website in a frame at the top, a set of navigation links in a narrow frame on the left, and the main content in large frame that occupies the rest of the page.

Disadvantages of Frames

The use of frames does have its own set of potential problems. For example, if a page that should be displayed in a frame is viewed without frames, there may not be navigation links available to get to other parts of the site. In addition, it is more difficult to print or bookmark a page within a frameset.

Framesets

A *frameset* stores information about the layout and properties of the frames used on a web page. The information includes the number of frames, their size, placement, and the web page that is displayed initially in each frame. This information will be used by the browser to lay out a web page.

Predefined Frameset Templates

Predefined frameset templates are available in Dreamweaver to create web page layouts quickly. Creating a document from a predefined frameset template or inserting a predefined frameset into a document will create all the framesets and frames needed to lay out the page.

The FRAMES Panel

The *FRAMES panel* provides a visual representation of the arrangement of frames on a web page. Each frame on the page is represented in the panel by its name surrounded by a border. Groups of frames are surrounded by thick borders. You can select a single frame, multiple frames, or the entire frameset by clicking the appropriate border.

Frame Properties

Frame properties allow you to enhance the appearance of frames on a web page. These properties can be set using the **PROPERTIES** panel. The following table describes the properties.

Property	Used To Specify
Scroll	The availability of scroll bars for a frame.
No resize	The visitor's ability to resize a frame.
Borders	The availability of border for a frame.
Border color	Color for the frame's border.
Margin width	The amount of space in pixels for the left and right margins of the frame.
Margin height	The amount of space in pixels for the top and bottom margins of the frame.

How to Create Framesets

Procedure Reference: Create a Frameset

To create a frameset:

1. Choose **File→New.**
2. In the **New Document** dialog box, select the **Page from Sample** category.
3. In the **Sample Folder** list box, select **Frameset.**
4. In the **Sample Page** list box, select the desired frameset.
5. Click **Create** to create a frameset.
6. In the **Frame Tag Accessibility Attributes** dialog box, specify a title for each frame.
    a. From the **Frame** drop-down list, select a frame.
    b. If necessary, in the **Title** text box, double-click and type a title for the frame.
    c. Click **OK.**
7. If necessary, resize the frames as required.
8. If necessary, on the **Document** toolbar, in the **Title** text box, modify the title of the web page.
9. If necessary, enter a name for each frame in the frameset.
    a. Choose **Window→Frames.**
    b. In the **Frames** panel, select a frame.
    c. In the **PROPERTIES** panel, in the **Frame name** text box, double-click and type the desired name for the frame.
10. Choose **File→Save Frameset As.**
11. If necessary, in the **Save As** dialog box, navigate to the desired folder.
12. In the **File name** text box, type a file name for the frameset.
13. Click **Save** to save the frameset.

Procedure Reference: Populating the Frames in a Frameset

To populate the frames in a frameset:

1. Open the frameset file that you created.

2. Add content to the frames in the frameset.
   - Load an existing web page in a frame.
     a. In the **Frames** panel, select the desired frame.
     b. In the **PROPERTIES** panel, using the **Src** property, load an existing web page.
       - To the right of the **Src** text box, click the **Browse for File** button, and in the **Select HTML File** dialog box, select the desired file.
       - To the right of the **Src** text box, drag the **Point to File** button to the desired file in the **FILES** panel or;
       - Click in the **Src** text box and type the path to the desired file.
   - Create a web page in a frame.
     a. In the document window, click in a frame.
     b. Add text, images, and other required elements in the frame.
     c. If necessary, choose **Modify→Page Properties** and in the **Page Properties** dialog box, modify the page properties.
     d. Choose **File→Save Frame As** and save the frame with an appropriate name.

3. Choose **File→Save All** to save the changes.

Procedure Reference: Link Frames

To link frames:

1. Select the desired text or image in a frame.

2. Link the selected text or image to the desired page.

3. In the **PROPERTIES** panel, from the **Target** drop-down list, select the desired option to set the target for the link page.

4. Choose **File→Save All** to save the frame links.

Options in the Target Drop-Down List

The **Target** drop-down list provides four options. The following table describes the options.

Option	Description
_blank	Creates a browser window and displays the linked web page in it.
_parent	Loads the linked web page into the current frame. It is the default value.
_self	Targets the entire browser window, removes all existing framesets, and loads the linked page in the current window.
_top	Targets the entire browser window and removes only the frameset that directly contains the current frame.

Procedure Reference: Set Frameset Properties

To set frameset properties:

1. In the **FRAMES** panel, click the border of the frameset to select it.
2. In the **PROPERTIES** panel, in the **RowCol Selection** section, select the desired row or column of the frameset.
3. Specify the size of the selected row or column.
   - In the **Row** section, in the **Value** text box, type a number and press **Enter** or;
   - In the **Column** section, in the **Value** text box, type a number and press **Enter.**
4. From the **Units** drop-down list, select the desired unit.
5. If necessary, in the **Border width** text box, double-click and type a number to specify the size of the border.
6. If necessary, from the **Borders** drop-down list, select the required option.
7. If necessary, in the **Border color** text box, type a color value for the border.
8. Choose **File→Save Frameset** to save the properties of the frameset.

Procedure Reference: Set Frame Properties

To set frame properties:

1. In the **FRAMES** panel, select the desired frame.
2. In the **PROPERTIES** panel, modify the selected frame's properties.
   - Double-click in the **Frame name** text box and type a name for the frame.
   - From the **Scroll** drop-down list, select the desired scrolling option.
   - In the **Margin width** text box, enter a value to set the margin width of the frame.
   - In the **Margin height** text box, enter a value to set the margin height of the frame.
   - Check the **No resize** check box to disable viewers from resizing the frame in their browser windows.
   - From the **Borders** drop-down list, select the desired option.
   - In the **Border color** text box, type a color value for the border.
3. Choose **File→Save All** to save the changes.

ACTIVITY A-1
Creating a Frameset

Data Files:

heading.html, body.html

Scenario:

You uploaded the web pages of the website. As you navigate through them, you realize that it would be helpful if the content in certain regions remained the same across all the pages, while the content in a few other regions changed per the visitors' requests.

---

1.   Create a web page with frames.

   a.   Choose **File→New.**

   b.   In the **New Document** dialog box, select the **Page from Sample** category.

   c.   In the **Sample Folder** list box, select **Frameset.**

   d.   In the **Sample Page** list box, select **Fixed Top, Nested Left** and click **Create** to create the frameset.

---

2.   Modify the accessibility attributes of the frames.

   a.   In the **Frame Tag Accessibility Attributes** dialog box, in the **Frame** drop-down list, verify that **mainFrame** is selected.

   b.   In the **Title** text box, double-click and type *main*

   c.   From the **Frame** drop-down list, select **topFrame.**

   d.   Double-click in the **Title** text box and type *header*

   e.   Similarly, assign the title *links* to **leftFrame.**

   f.   Click **OK.**

---

3.   Modify the title and save the frameset page.

   a.   On the **Document** toolbar, in the **Title** text box, click before the word "Untitled," hold down **Shift,** and click after the word "Document" to select both words.

   b.   Press **Delete** and type *Our Global Company*

   c.   Choose **File→Save Frameset.**

   d.   In the **Save As** dialog box, navigate to the C:\084502Data\Working with Framesets\ Our Global Company folder.

   e.   In the **File name** text box, click and type *index2.html* and then click **Save** to save the frameset.

---

4.   Insert web pages in the **topFrame** and **mainFrame.**

---

a. Choose **Window→Frames.**

b. In the **FRAMES** panel, select **topFrame.**

c. In the **PROPERTIES** panel, to the right of the **Src** text box, click the **Browse for File** button.

d. In the **Select HTML File** dialog box, navigate to the C:\084502Data\Working with Framesets\Our Global Company folder.

e. In the **Select HTML File** dialog box, select **heading.html** and click **OK.**

f. Observe that the heading.html page appears in the top frame of the frameset.

g. Link the **mainFrame** to the body.html file.

h. In the document window, click in the left frame.

i. Choose **File→Save Frame.**

j. In the **Save As** dialog box, navigate to the C:\084502Data\Working with Framesets\ Our Global Company folder.

k. In the **File name** text box, click and type *links.html* and click **Save** to save the frameset.

---

5. Resize the left and top frames.

a. In the **FRAMES** panel, click the border surrounding **leftFrame** and **mainFrame** to select both the frames.

b. In the **PROPERTIES** panel, in the **RowCol Selection** box, verify that the left column is selected.

c. In the **Column** section, double-click in the **Value** text box, type *138* and press **Enter.**

d. In the **FRAMES** panel, click the border surrounding all the frames to select the entire frameset.

e. In the **PROPERTIES** panel, in the **RowCol Selection** box, verify that the top row is selected.

f. In the **Row** section, double-click in the **Value** text box, type *90* and press **Enter.**

---

6. Set the frame properties for **leftFrame.**

a. In the document window, click in the left frame.

b. In the **PROPERTIES** panel, click **Page Properties.**

c. In the **Category** list box, verify that **Appearance (CSS)** is selected.

d. In the **Appearance (CSS)** section, click in the **Background color** text box and type *#4C70A2*

e. Click in the **Left margin** text box, type *0* and press **Tab** twice.

f. In the **Right margin** text box, type *0* and press **Tab** twice.

g. In the **Top margin** text box, type *90* and in the **Bottom margin** text box, type *0*

h. Click **OK.**

---

7. Preview the web page in a browser.

   a. Choose **File→Save All** to save all the frames and the frameset file.

   b. On the **Document** toolbar, click the **Preview/Debug in browser** button and choose **Preview in IExplore** to preview the web page in Internet Explorer.

   c. Close the browser window.

B | Using Dreamweaver Extensions

Dreamweaver Extensions

Dreamweaver extensions refer to software that can be added to the Dreamweaver application to enhance its capabilities. Some of these extensions allow for reformatting of tables, writing a script for a browser, or connecting to back-end databases. Extensions can be installed, managed, and removed using Adobe® Extension Manager CS5, which can be accessed from Dreamweaver. Adobe® Extension Manager CS5 can be launched from the **Help** menu or using the **Extend Dreamweaver** button on the Application bar.

C | New Features in Adobe Dreamweaver CS5

The following table lists the new features pertaining to Adobe® Dreamweaver® CS5 and where those new features are covered in this course. For example, 1-A indicates that the feature is addressed in Lesson 1, Topic A.

Feature	Adobe® Dreamweaver® CS5: Level 1	Adobe® Dreamweaver® CS5: Level 2	Adobe® Dreamweaver® CS5: Level 3
New User Interface (The Site Setup Dialog Box)	Lesson 2 Topic C		
Use of Adobe BrowserLab	Lesson 1 Topic A, Lesson 6 Topic A		
CSS Enable/Disable	Lesson 3 Topic B		
Linguistic Library Optimized	Lesson 2 Topic D		
Starter Layouts		To be covered in level 2	
CSS Inspection		To be covered in level 2	
CSS Incremental Pagination		To be covered in level 2	
Dynamic Related Files and Live View			To be covered in level 3
Live Changes			To be covered in level 3
Subversion Enhancements			To be covered in level 3
Adobe Widget Browser		To be covered in level 2	
InContext Editing	Lesson 3 Topic B		

Lesson Labs

Lesson labs are provided as an additional learning resource for this course. The labs may or may not be performed as part of the classroom activities. Your instructor will consider setup issues, classroom timing issues, and instructional needs to determine which labs are appropriate for you to perform, and at what point during the class. If you do not perform the labs in class, your instructor can tell you if you can perform them independently as self-study, and if there are any special setup requirements.

Lesson 1 Lab 1

Preparing to Use the Dreamweaver Interface

Data Files:

index.html

Scenario:

You want to provide information about your country on a website. You decide to create a website, using the Adobe Dreamweaver application. Before proceeding with the task, you want to be thorough with the location and functionality of the application's interface elements. Also, you want to modify the interface so that the required tools can be accessed easily.

1. Open the Adobe Dreamweaver application.

2. From the C:\084502Data\Getting Started with Dreamweaver\Citizens Info folder, open the index.html file.

3. In the **INSERT** panel, from the drop-down list, select the various categories to view their options.

4. Close the **AP ELEMENTS** panel.

5. Dock the **CSS STYLES** panel to the left of the document window.

6. Group the **ASSETS** panel with the **CSS STYLES** panel.

7. Save the workspace layout as *Customized.*

8. Close the index.html file.

Lesson 2 Lab 1

Initiating a Website

Data Files:

Introduction.txt

Scenario:

The structure of the Citizens Info site is defined. As you develop the site further, you want the files to be accessible through Dreamweaver to maintain the structure of the site. You also want to create a home page using the information provided in the Introduction.txt file.

---

1. Define a site named **Citizens Info** and specify the local root folder location as C:\ 084502Data\Initiating a Website\Citizens Info. Set the remote server connection method to **None.**

---

2. Modify the site definition to specify the default images folder location as C:\Student\ Initiating a Website\Citizens Info\images.

---

3. Create a blank HTML document and set the title as **Citizens Information Center.**

---

4. Include **Citizens Information Center, Chermont, community** as the keywords and **Dedicated to bringing people together** as the description.

---

5. In the document, add the text from the Introduction.txt file and remove the empty paragraphs.

---

6. Save the document as **index.html.**

Lesson 3 Lab 1

Creating Web Pages

Data Files:

index.html, info-center.html, privacy.html, copyrights.html, banner.gif, Copyrights.doc, terms.html, news.jpg, communities.gif

Before You Begin:

Specify the folder location for the Citizens Info site using data from the C:\084502Data\ Designing Web Pages\Citizens Info folder.

Scenario:

You are designing web pages for the Citizens Information Center site. You need to ensure that the content on your site pages is properly formatted. On the Information Center page, you want to include a banner of the site and provide information about the seasonal temperature in Chermont city. In addition, your co-worker has provided copyright information in a Word document and the Privacy Policy in a HTML file and has requested that you include these on the site. As these files were created using Word, you need to ensure that both the files contain proper HTML markup tags.

---

1. In the index.html file, apply the **Heading 1** heading format for the text "Our Community" and specify the CSS heading properties using the following settings:
    - Font type: **Arial, Helvetica, sans-serif**
    - Font size: **15**
    - Font color: **#001A5C**

---

2. Create a container surrounding the text and specify the ID as *leftcol.*

---

3. Create an ID style named *#leftcol* and in the **Box** category, specify the following settings:
    - **Width**: *500* pixels
    - **Float: left**
    - Padding for **Top**: *5* pixels

---

4. In the info-center.html file, under the heading "Community Facilities," format the items as an unordered list.

---

5. At the top of the page, in the container for the header, insert the banner.gif image from the **images** folder and set the alternate text to *Citizens Information Center.*

---

6. Below the heading "Climate in Chermont," create a table with 3 rows, 3 columns, and specify the following settings:
   - **Table width:** *433* pixels
   - **Border thickness:** *0*
   - **Cell padding:** *0*
   - **Cell spacing:** *0*

7. In the table, specify the following information.

Seasons	*Temp (in Fahrenheit)*	*Temp (in Celsius)*
Avg. Winter Temp	25.00 F	-3.89 C
Avg. Summer Temp	75.40 F	24.11 C

8. Create a class style named *.thead* and set the following CSS properties:
   - (Type category) Font-family: **Arial, Helvetica, sans-serif**
   - (Type category) Font-size: **14**
   - (Type category) Font-weight: **Bold**
   - (Background category) Background-color: *#99CCFF*
   - (Block category) Text-align: **Center**

9. Create a class style named *.tbody* and set the following CSS properties:
   - Font-family: **Arial, Helvetica, sans-serif**
   - Font-size: **14**
   - Background-color: *#EFEFEF*
   - Text-align: **Center**

10. Apply the *.thead* class style to the first row and the **.tbody** class style to the last two rows.

11. Open the privacy.html file and clean up the word HTML.

12. Move the news.jpg and communities.gif files to the images folder.

13. Create a subfolder named *Legal* and move the copyrights.html, privacy.html, and terms.html files to it.

Lesson 4 Lab 1

Using Reusable Site Assets

Data Files:

index.html, info-center.html, announcement.txt, pagelayout.html, boardmeetings.html, meetings.txt

Before You Begin:

Define the Citizens Info site using data from the C:\084502Data\Creating Reusable Site Assets\ Citizens Info folder.

Scenario:

You have worked on web pages for your site. You notice that the footer information needs to be changed, and the news headlines that scroll across the site need to be updated. You also need to include an additional event in the upcoming events page.

1. Save important announcements in the index.html file as a library item named **announcements.**

2. Insert the **announcements** library item in the right column of the info-center.html file.

3. In the **announcements** library item, remove the first announcement, add a new announcement that is given in the announcement.txt file, and update the change on all pages.

4. Save the footer information in the index.html file as a snippet and name it **footer_info** in the **Citizens Info.**

5. Insert the **footer_info** snippet in the info-center.html and pagelayout.html files as the footer.

6. Save the pagelayout.html file as a template file, with the option to add more rows of data to the table.

7. Use the template to create a file named **boardmeetings.html,** and add the information from the meetings.txt file to the table.

8. Save and close all the files.

Lesson 5 Lab 1

Links

Data Files:

index.html, info-center.html, contact-info.html, copyrights.html, privacy.html, terms.html, home.jpg, home_down.jpg, information center.jpg, information center_down.jpg, news room.jpg, news room_down.jpg, contact us_down.jpg

Before You Begin:

1. Ensure that you have an email account configured in the email client installed on your computer.
2. Define the Citizens Info site using data from the C:\084502Data\Working with Links\Citizens Info folder.
3. Add the C:\084502Data\Working with Links\Citizens Info\images folder as the default images folder.
4. Open index.html file.

Scenario:

You designed the necessary web pages for your site. You also need to provide proper page navigation to ensure that information is easily accessible for the site visitors.

---

1. Link the text "Trademark & Copyright" to the copyrights.html file within the Legal folder.

---

2. Similarly, link the text "Privacy Policy" and "Terms and Conditions" to the privacy.html and terms.html files within the Legal folder, respectively.

---

3. Save the index.html file.

---

4. Open the info-center.html file.

---

5. In the info-center.html file, create an anchor named *top* for the heading "Information Center."

---

6. Create an anchor named *community* for the heading "Major Service Providers of our Community."

---

7. Save and close the info-center.html file.

---

8. At the bottom of the page, link the text "Top" to the anchor "top."

---

9. In the index.html file, link the text "Click here" to the anchor "community" in the info-center.html file.

10. In the index.html file, on the image in the right column container, create a rectangular hotspot surrounding the text "Dedicated to bringing people together to discuss issues that are important in their communities." Set the alternate text to **Community Information Center** and link it to the info-center.html file.

11. Create a rollover effect for the navigation menu images, using the following information.

Image Name	Original Image	Rollover Image	Alternate Text	Link
Home	home.jpg	home_down.jpg	Home	index.html
Information Center	information center.jpg	information center_down.jpg	Information Center	info-center.html
News room	news room.jpg	news room_down.jpg	News room	newsroom.html
Contact Us	contact us.jpg	contact us_down.jpg	Contact us	contact-info.html

12. Save and close the index.html file.

13. In the contact-info.html file, create an email link for the text "james_r@citizensinfo.org."

14. Preview the file.

Lesson 6 Lab 1

Uploading a Website

Data Files:

newsroom.html, index.html

Before You Begin:

Define the Citizens Info site using data from the C:\084502Data\Uploading a Website\Citizens Info folder.

Scenario:

You designed your website. Now, you want to check for broken links and target browser compatibility, validate site reports, and rectify errors before uploading the website to your local site folder.

---

1. Open the newsroom.html file and validate it against the XHTML 1.0 Transitional tag library.

---

2. Set the target browser as Internet Explorer 7.0 and check the home page for browser compatibility.

---

3. Generate site reports for the **Missing Alt Text** option for the entire current local site.

---

4. Correct the error shown in the index.html file.

---

5. Check for broken links, external links, and orphaned files for the entire current local site.

---

6. In the index.html file, correct the broken link to the newsroom.html file.

---

7. Edit the site definition by selecting **FTP** as the remote access method.

---

8. Specify *172.30.4.197* as the FTP host and *Student[ID]* as the Host directory, and test the remote connection.

---

9. Upload the files to the FTP location, and in the expanded **FILES** panel, view the remote files.

Appendix A Lab 1

Working with Frames

Data Files:

header.html, sidemenu.html, content.html, info.html, news.html, contact.html, Home_over.jpg, Home_up.jpg, Information Center_up.jpg, Information Center_over.jpg, Contact Us_over.jpg, Contact Us_up.jpg, Newsroom_over.jpg, Newsroom_up.jpg

Before You Begin:

Define the Citizens Info site using data from the C:\084502Data\Working with Framesets\ Citizens Info folder.

Scenario:

You want to have the header and navigation bars on all the pages of your website. You also want to vary the content on the other parts of a page depending on the link selected.

1. Create a **Fixed Top, Nested Left** frameset.

2. Specify the title attribute of **mainFrame** as *Content,* **leftFrame** as *Sidemenu,* and **topFrame** as *Header.*

3. Modify the frame name of **mainFrame** as *maincontent* and **leftFrame** as *sidemenu.*

4. Save the frameset as *citizensinfo.html.*

5. Link the **topFrame** to **header.html,** the **sidemenu** frame to **sidemenu.html,** and the **maincontent** frame to **content.html.**

6. In the frameset, set the **Value** for **topFrame** to *140* pixels and the **Value** for **sidemenu** to *192* pixels.

7. In the **sidemenu** frame, create a navigation bar with links to the **Home, Information Center, News Room,** and **Contact Us** pages. Use the images with corresponding names in up and over states to create rollover effects for the links.

8. In the **sidemenu** frame, select each link and set the target to the **maincontent** frame.

9. Save the web page and preview it in a browser.

Solutions

Lesson 1

Activity 1-1

1. **What does the first part of a URL indicate?**

    a) IP address

    b) Domain name

    c) File name

    ✓ d) Protocol

2. **Which statement is true about websites?**

    a) A website can contain only one web page.

    b) The web pages on a website cannot be linked through images.

    ✓ c) A website is accessed using its URL.

    d) Websites can contain information only in the form of text.

3. **True or False? Before creating a website, you need to identify the audience who will be visiting the site.**

    ✓ True

    ___ False

Activity 1-2

2. **Which component in the Dreamweaver interface provides information about the magnification level of a document?**

    ✓ a) The status bar

    b) The document window

    c) The PROPERTIES panel

    d) The Document toolbar

4. **When would you use the PROPERTIES panel?**

   a) To switch between different views to view a document.

   b) To open a new document.

   c) To view the size of the current document.

   ✓ d) To modify the properties of objects such as text and graphics.

Lesson 2

Activity 2-1

1. **Which definition best describes a project plan deliverable?**

   a) The list of resources and tools required for a project.

   b) The performance measurements of a project.

   ✓ c) The outcome of a project phase or the outcome of a project.

   d) The sequential phases of a project life cycle.

2. **Identify the plans that are used as supporting project plans.**

   ✓ a) Communication plan

   ✓ b) Risk management plan

   c) Workflow plan

   ✓ d) Resource plan

Activity 2-2

1. **Which definition best describes a storyboard?**

   a) It is a visual representation of a website.

   b) It defines the navigation logic of a website.

   ✓ c) It is a series of sketches that depict the rough appearance of the pages of a website.

   d) It is a document that contains one or more sketches that depict all of the potential directions in which a website may be navigated through.

2. **True or False? A site map is an image of the appearance of a web page.**

   ___ True

   ✓ False

Lesson 3

Activity 3-1

1. What is an embedded style?

   ✓ a) A type of CSS that is defined in the head section using the <style> tag.

      b) A set of class styles that can be applied to any element on a page.

      c) A type of CSS that is applied directly to tags on a web page using the style attribute.

      d) A CSS file that is attached to a web page.

2. What is a tag style?

      a) A CSS style that is saved as a separate CSS file and attached to a web page.

   ✓ b) A CSS style that can be applied to a particular tag on a page.

      c) A CSS style that can be applied to multiple elements on a page.

      d) A CSS style that can be applied directly to tags on a web page using the style attribute.

3. Which of these are types of CSS?

   ✓ a) Inline style

      b) Class style

   ✓ c) Embedded style

   ✓ d) External style

Activity 3-4

1. Which term describes the illegal use of a copyrighted work?

      a) Fair use doctrine

      b) Copyrightable work

   ✓ c) Infringement

      d) Derivative work

2. Which elements will you use as part of a copyright notice? (Choose three.)

   ✓ a) The copyright symbol (©).

      b) The country of the copyright registration.

   ✓ c) The word "copyright."

   ✓ d) The phrase "All Rights Reserved."

Lesson 5

Activity 5-3

3. **True or False? Email links can be created only for text.**

    ___ True

    ✓ False

Glossary

Adobe CSS Advisor
A website that provides information, suggestions, and tips on the latest browser and code issues in Dreamweaver.

anchor
A link that takes users to a particular location on a page.

CSS rule
A rule that describes styles applied to an element on a web page.

CSS
(Cascading Style Sheets) A collection of rules that define the style applied to specific elements.

div tag
A block-level element that is used to define logical sections on a web page.

domain name
A unique textual name used to access a website on the Internet.

flowchart
A more powerful and detailed way to map out a website's flow, taking various navigation options into account.

FRAMES panel
Provides a visual representation of the arrangement of frames on a web page.

frames
Used to lay out a web page by dividing the browser window into multiple regions.

frameset
Used to store information about the layout and properties of a set of frames used on a web page.

Get command
Used to copy files from a remote site to a local site.

GIF
(Graphic Interchange Format) A graphic file format that is limited to 256 colors and, therefore, is most useful for images with a few colors or with large areas of flat colors.

guide
A reference line used to position and align objects in a document.

home page
The entry point of a website, providing access to other pages on the site.

hotspot
An area on an image that can be clicked to open a linked web page.

HTTP
(HyperText Transfer Protocol) The standard protocol used to access websites.

hyperlinks
Links that reference another web page on the same website or a different website.

image map
A single image that contains multiple hotspots, which can be clicked to open a linked web page.

IP address
A numeric address that helps identify a computer on the Internet.

JPEG
(Joint Photographic Experts Group) A graphic file format that uses compression to dramatically reduce the file size of images, thus allowing for faster download and display.

library
A file that is used to store objects that can be used later on web pages.

lists
Display information in a structured and organized format.

lossless compression
A compression that maintains image resolution when the image size is increased.

lossy compression
A compression that can result in pixilated images when the image size is increased.

nested tables
Tables that are placed within a cell.

Panel groups
Groups of related panels.

PNG
(Portable Network Graphic) A graphic file format that supports more than 256 colors along with transparency.

project deliverables
The output of any phase of a project or the entire project.

project plan
A plan that defines the execution of a project and the management of the processes and resources of the plan.

Put command
Used to upload files from a local site to a remote site.

Results panel group
A panel group that contains tools that you can use to search for information and validate web pages for accessibility and browser compatibility issues.

rollover
An element on a web page that provides visual feedback and facilitates navigation through a web page.

rulers
Visual aids that display graded units of measurements, which appear at the top and left edges of the document window in Design view.

scope creep
Change in the scope of a project after commencement of the project.

site maps
A representation of the structure of a website.

Site Setup dialog box
A dialog box that is used to define a website.

SNIPPETS panel
A panel that allows you to view and manage snippets on a website.

snippets
Blocks of code that are stored for use on other web pages.

span tag
An inline element that is used to format other inline elements.

spry framework
A framework developed by Adobe and integrated into Dreamweaver, that is used to create animation effects, data, and widgets.

spry interface widget
A graphical interface element of the Adobe spry framework that is used to display data and enable user interaction on a web page.

storyboard
One or more sketches depicting the rough appearance and flow of web pages, including navigation elements that allow the user to interact.

tables

Structured formats that allow presentation of data in grids of rows and columns.

tag styles

CSS styles applied to individual tags to redefine tags' properties.

template

A document that contains predefined design elements such as graphics and text.

URL

(Uniform Resource Locator) The unique address for a file that is accessible on the Internet.

validator preferences

The settings that apply to the Dreamweaver validator.

website

A set of interconnected web pages displayed on the Internet.

XHTML

(eXtensible HyperText Markup Language) A markup language that is a reformulation of HTML and is used to create a web page.

Index

frames, 176
  linking, 178
  populating in a frameset, 178
framesets
  creating, 177

G

general preferences
  setting, 22
Graphic Interchange Format
  See: GIF

H

home pages, 41
hotspots, 141
HTML websites
  defining, 36
hyperlinks, 127
  creating, 129

I

image maps
  creating, 142
image properties
  setting, 75
images
  editing in Fireworks, 74
  inserting on a page, 74
  scaling, 75
import commands in Dreamweaver, 89

J

Joint Photographic Experts Group
  See: JPEG

L

libraries, 101
library items
  creating, 103
  deleting, 104
  modifying, 107
  placing on site pages, 104
  renaming, 104
links on the site
  checking, 165
links to a deleted file
  updating, 167
links to the file

updating, 167
lists, 55
lossy compression, 71

M

menus
  Format, 54

O

options
  Favorites, 101
  Site, 101

P

Page size resolution, 40
pages from a template
  creating, 116
Panel groups, 19
panels
  ASSETS, 101
  CSS STYLES, 55
  FILES, 36
  FRAMES, 176
  INSERT, 57
  PROPERTIES, 54
  SITE REPORTS, 159
  SNIPPETS, 111
Portable Network Graphic
  See: PNG
project deliverables, 30
project plans
  phases of, 29

R

regions in a template
  defining, 116
Results panel group, 158
rollovers
  creating, 147

S

site definition information
  editing, 36
site files
  updating, 168
site maps, 33
site reports
  generating, 160